ANALYZING COMPUTER ARCHITECTURES

ANALYZING
Computer Architectures

Jerome C. Huck and Michael J. Flynn

IEEE COMPUTER SOCIETY NUMBER 857
LIBRARY OF CONGRESS NUMBER 88-45744
IEEE CATALOG NUMBER EH0285-7
ISBN 0-8186-8857-2

IEEE COMPUTER SOCIETY

THE INSTITUTE OF ELECTRICAL AND ELECTRONICS ENGINEERS, INC.

COMPUTER SOCIETY PRESS

ANALYZING COMPUTER ARCHITECTURES

Jerome C. Huck
Michael J. Flynn

IEEE Computer Society Press

Washington • Los Alamitos • Belgium • Tokyo

Published by IEEE Computer Society Press
1730 Massachusetts Avenue, N.W.
Washington, D.C. 20036-1903

Cover designed by Jack I. Ballestero

Copyright © 1989 by The Institute of Electrical and Electronics Engineers, Inc.

Printed in the United States of America

All rights reserved. No part of this book may be reproduced in any form including photostat, microfilm, and xerography, and not in information storage and retrieval systems, without permission in writing from the publisher, except by a reviewer who may quote brief passages in a review or as provided in the Copyright Act of 1976.

QA
76.9
.A73   /73141
H83
1989

IEEE Computer Society Order Number 857
Library of Congress Number 88-45744
IEEE Catalog Number EH0285-7
ISBN 0-8186-8857-2 (casebound)
ISBN 0-8186-4857-0 (microfiche)
SAN 264-620X

Additional copies may be ordered from:

IEEE Computer Society	IEEE Service Center	IEEE Computer Society	IEEE Computer Society
10662 Los Vaqueros Circle	445 Hoes Lane	13, Avenue de l'Aquilon	Ooshima Building
Los Alamitos, CA	P.O. Box 1331	B-1200 Brussels	2-19-1 Minami-Aoyama,
90720-2578	Piscataway, NJ	BELGIUM	Minato-Ku
	08855-1331		Tokyo 107 JAPAN

THE INSTITUTE OF ELECTRICAL AND ELECTRONICS ENGINEERS, INC.

Preface

This work is a study of instruction sets and their effectiveness. The instruction set forms a specification for a computer designer. It represents the universe of what must be implemented or realized. While many implementation variations are possible, the instruction set is a primary determinant of the ultimate cost–performance ratio that is realized by the designer. However, since it is difficult to measure the effectiveness of an instruction set it can become a center of controversy.

The hierarchical nature of the computing process creates some of the difficulty in isolating effects. Applications written in higher level languages are translated by compilers into object code. This object code is a symbolic form of the instruction set, and is executed by the processor. The effectiveness of the execution of the application depends upon:

1. The compiler.

2. The instruction set.

3. The implementation of the instruction set.

It is difficult to measure the effectiveness of one of these dimensions (e.g., the instruction set) since the other dimensions are closely dependent on it.

The purpose of this book is to provide a study of the effectiveness of instruction sets. To this end we present methodologies, data, interpretation, and finally, observations on a spectrum of contemporary machines. Fundamental to this book are the data. The data are derived from running a suite of benchmark programs on a number of machines and from measuring implementation-independent effects (numbers of instructions, program size, etc.) under controlled compiler conditions.

In any effort to control many variables such as compiler and implementation, there must be limitations. The data are collected based on a limited number of benchmarks. It is for single processor (single instruction counter) style computers, and hence few issues in concurrency are studied. The benchmarks are user-oriented, as distinct from systems code.

The monograph is intended for the computer professional or advanced student. It is a monograph and not a text. The reader is presumed

 AUGUSTANA UNIVERSITY COLLEGE
LIBRARY

to be familiar with machines such as IBM Systems 360 and 370, VAX, RISC architectures, and variations thereof.

The presentation of data can be either exciting or boring, depending upon the reader's eye. In order to make the material a bit more generally accessible, we have adopted a "presentation plus observation" style. That is, in the basic text of the monograph, the data (also abstracted in Huck [36]), its motivation and methodology are presented with straightforward interpretation. This is supplemented with boxed insets which represent observations, conclusions, or summary statements that help highlight the applications of the material for the more casual reader.

These data are an outgrowth of work done in the Stanford Emulation Laboratory and some of the data were presented in a thesis by J. C. Huck, "Comparative Analysis of Computer Architectures." This book extends the data presented in the thesis by including analysis of VAX/VMS, the HP Precision Architecture, and the Architect's Workbench data.

We are pleased to acknowledge the efforts of many of our colleagues in supporting the environment that allowed us to make the measurements presented herein, especially Dr. Charles Neuhauser, who was an early contributor to the establishment of the emulation facility, Drs. Chad Mitchell and Hans Mulder, who built early versions of the Architect's Workbench, Kathy Cuderman who helped us gather some of the data presented here, Andrew Zimmerman, Brian Bray, and Alan Kobrin, who contributed to the evolution of the Architect's Workbench tool system, and finally Susan Gere, who worked tirelessly to organize and design the final version of the manuscript.

Michael Flynn

Jerome Huck

Palo Alto, California
April 1989

AUGUSTANA UNIVERSITY COLLEGE
LIBRARY

Contents

List of Figures

List of Tables

ANALYZING COMPUTER ARCHITECTURES

Chapter 1

Introduction

Chapter 1: Introduction

Computer comparisons examine the effectiveness of different designs by analyzing their performance on user programs. These programs may be expressed in different languages, and are translated or compiled into a final representation—the machine code—that can be executed by the computer system or the "machine."

A machine has three components: a set of commands, called the *instruction set*, a *storage*, and an *interpretive mechanism* [22]. A machine's storage consists of all objects distinguishable by the instruction set in which a value can be saved and later retrieved. The combination of instruction set and storage objects defines the *architecture* of a machine. The interpretive mechanism *executes* a program by causing transformations in the storage of a machine.

The interpretive mechanism can itself be a machine. That is, it can have its own instruction set, its own storage (perhaps larger than the original storage), and its own interpretive mechanism. The hierarchy of machines is distinguished by defining a machine at a higher level, the *image* machine, and a machine that acts as the interpretive mechanism, the *host* machine (Figure 1.1). The program that executes on the host is called an *interpreter* or *emulator*. The components of a host machine are often distinguished by the prefix *micro* and termed *microinstructions*, *microstorage*, and *micromachine*.

Often the interpretive mechanism is designed for a specific image machine and many special functions are included. A machine not directed to any particular image, but designed to emulate a variety of architectures, is called a *universal* host. A universal host, while not as high-performance as a dedicated host, allows the emulation of several different, and perhaps unimplemented, architectures on a single host.

This book compares architectures by measuring the execution of two identical sets of high-level-language programs; these programs are called the *work load*. The analysis relies on observable measures that reflect the effectiveness of an instruction set. With other factors being equal, an architecture that requires fewer instructions to execute a program is superior. Other measures include: storage requirements, execution times, and the complexity of the interpretation. The measurements must be accurately gathered. If a compiler causes a machine

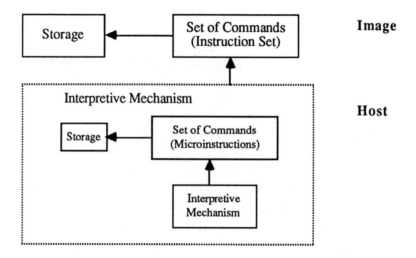

Figure 1.1: Image and host machines.

to clear the storage area before starting program execution, then these instructions should not be included in a comparison to another machine whose compiler does not clear storage.

The measures can include factors not related to the architecture. The major unrelated component is the compiler. The machine code representation produced by the compiler may not be the *best* representation for a particular architecture. To compare fairly, it is necessary to understand how the compilation process affects the instruction stream. This book examines the role of the compiler and measures its effects.

The study and comparison of machine architectures is motivated by many factors. Instruction sets are the interface between the interpretive mechanism and an algorithm, and as such contribute greatly to the performance of the system. The interpreter attempts to execute an instruction sequence as fast as possible. When the architecture is simpler, the interpreter can likely run faster or be implemented at a lower cost. This improvement may be offset by an increase in the number of machine code instructions needed to represent the program. The converse situation can also occur. Several simple instructions could be combined to produce a smaller representation, but the interpreter could increase in cost or decrease in speed. These choices are very sensitive to current implementation technology.

Advances in the field of integrated circuits has changed many of the constraints used to design architectures. Previously, the cost of *computation* dominated design decisions. More recently, the cost of *communication* is emerging as a principal bottleneck to higher-speed machines.

In the past, computer architects largely concentrated on implementation issues in instruction set design. Advances in compiler technology require the re-evaluation of many design tradeoffs, especially the inclusion of the compiler as an integral part of instruction set design.

1.1:   Previous Work

The first architectural studies evaluated a single instruction set. Often a study required developing new techniques in the area of instruction sequence *stream* measurement.

High-level-language execution studies have been primarily directed at determining the language constructs most frequently used. The earliest work used only the program representation, a static analysis, and was directed at providing information to language designers. Later efforts examined the actual execution of the program, a dynamic analysis, to aid architectural decisions. These studies recognize that high-level-language programs (in both compilation and execution) are the primary work load of contemporary machines.

Despite their obvious importance, architectural comparisons of meaningful scope are rarely found in the literature. Analyses performed by a manufacturer are considered proprietary data and remain internal reports. There is also considerable difficulty in establishing an environment for comparative analysis. It is necessary to have access to all the machines for a study, either in the form of simulators or the actual machine. A reasonable work load requires that I/O be supported without affecting the measurements. Further, a design in a commercial environment develops rapidly. This makes it difficult to conduct time-consuming experiments or to analyze results that could help the design.

1.1.1:   *Instruction Set Analysis and Measurement*

The earliest effort to measure and analyze instruction sets [26] examined the IBM 704 computer. The work was performed in 1959 and partitioned each executed instruction into one of 13 classes. This Gibson classification groups instructions into similar functions. The classes include: load/store, fixed-point add/subtract, compare, branch, multiply, and divide. Gibson reported that load and store operations account for roughly 38 percent of the instructions, branches for 20 percent, and fixed-point add/sub for 7 percent. An additional class was defined to count instructions that used an index register. The percentages reported here have been scaled to eliminate that class, to make this original study comparable to later studies that do not include indexing. Results from other studies were in general agreement with Gibson. The architectures included IBM S/370 [17,56,73], DEC PDP-10 [41], and CDC 3600 [27]. Rossmann's study of S/370, while generally in agreement, showed the wide variance in measurements due to the work load. The average load/store class fraction was 40 percent, but ranged from less than one in three to more than half of the instruction stream.

The early studies of instruction set execution were primarily aimed at helping the machine designer implement the architecture, while later studies were aimed at improving an architecture. Alexander [3] measured S/370 execution by having the compiler insert a trace instruction before each branch instruction. The work load included several student compiler projects plus a production compiler for the language XPL. The distribution of S/370 operations changed from earlier studies, as a greater fraction of the instructions moved data and the branch frequency dropped to 15 percent. This change is consistent with high-level-language results presented here.

Shustek [59] analyzed S/370 execution by first interpreting the machine code to produce a record (trace) of each instruction, and later by analyzing the trace. This study built a model of two high-performance implementations of the S/370 architecture, and analyzed the resource demands made by the instruction stream. The collected data include operation and operation pair distributions, branch analysis, operand address utilization, and operand information. Characteristics of other architectures were included to examine features not present in the S/370. This analysis in some cases was based only on static data. The conclusions recognized the influence of the compiler on a language-oriented machine (P-code), but did not expand this observation to better understand the S/370 instruction stream.

A study of the PDP-10 instruction set [41] uses an interpreter for the machine to collect dynamic statistics. The input to the interpreter consists of a program and a description of the machine, termed ISP. This study presents a detailed analysis of the instruction stream. An interesting result of this work was that register utilization was found to be low. Of 16 registers, an average of seven registers held data that were used later in the instruction stream. Also, a model for register use was created to determine the cost of a reduced register set. If the PDP-10 has only eight registers, then the instruction stream grows by less than 20 percent. These conclusions should be reevaluated in light of more recent compiler optimization advances (see Chapter 5).

A thorough study of the PDP-11 architecture [48] was performed to verify instruction measurement through emulation. The same mechanism as used in that study is used here and is discussed in Chapter 2.

CHAPTER 1. INTRODUCTION

Neuhauser examined both user programs and the operating system. The PDP-11 architecture was structured to allow arbitrary operation and operand combinations (called orthogonality). Neuhauser showed that orthogonality reduced the effectiveness of the architecture due to the infrequency of many combinations, and that the instruction stream was dominated by simple operations and operands.

Two studies of the VAX machine used different mechanisms to measure the instruction set. Wiecek [72] generated trace tapes by using a built-in instruction trace mechanism. Called the trace bit, the execution of each instruction forces an interrupt to another process that collects data. The study examined compiler execution and reported on the composition of typical instructions and operand specifiers. Many of the observations made by Neuhauser about the PDP-11 apply to the VAX architecture.

Clark [14,15] used a hardware monitor wired into the back-plane of a VAX machine. Opcode frequencies and timing information were collected. The rankings of the opcodes by frequency and execution time varied because of the different computational and referencing requirements of instructions. The CALL instruction accounted for 2.54 percent of the instructions, but required 22 percent of the execution time. The poor execution time is largely the result of the store-through cache used by the VAX 11/780. The two VAX studies were used to verify and compare results presented here.

Other studies have examined specific facets of machine architectures. Foster [24] analyzed the opcodes found in a CDC 3600 instruction stream. The costs and potential savings were then estimated to reencode the opcodes. He proposed a new mechanism that sets an internal state that determines the (conditional) interpretation of the next opcode. Traditional machines allow any operation to follow any other operation, yet many combinations do not occur. Opcode pair frequencies reported by other studies are another measure of this effect. A more recent architecture, the VAX, uses a limited form of conditional encoding. An escape opcode changes the interpretation of the next opcode to provide for infrequent operations.

Hammerstrom [29] studied the information content of the address stream of the S/370 architecture. A trace was made of the addresses generated by the instruction stream. The results showed that address calculations account for a large portion of all machine computations and the information content of the address stream is on the order of one or two bits per reference.

1.1.2: High-Level Language Execution and Measurement

The earliest study of programming language execution by Knuth [39] examined a collection of Fortran programs. The static analysis of the programs showed that very simple constructs were most frequently used. Assignment statements seldom had more than one operator, array indices were rarely expressions, and loop constructs often used constant bounds. The dynamic analysis used a different work load (small, student-written programs), so it was not possible to examine the changes in the dynamic and static use of a programming language. A study of commercial PL/I programs [20] and scientific Fortran programs [55] verified Knuth's results on the simple use of language constructs.

Wortman [74] studied the use of the language *Student/PL*, an introductory programming language and a subset of PL/I. The compiler produces machine code for a stack architecture called the Student/PL machine. Static language statistics were collected by modifying the compiler to count each language construct. From these data, Wortman redesigned the Student/PL machine to minimize program size. Dynamic measures were obtained by modifying the interpreter to collect various instruction statistics. These results were compared to the same work load executing on an S/370 machine. Unfortunately the compiler used for the S/370 execution, PL/I (F), generates very poor code and prevents any architectural comparisons. The work load included only beginning student programs and biased several of his conclusions.

Another study [66] extended Wortman's thesis by using dynamic language statistics in the design cycle. Tanenbaum recognized that the dynamic instruction stream differs from the static representation. Design decisions that reduce the size of a program might not apply to the dynamic instruction stream.

Other studies have examined specific facets of high-level-language execution. Patterson [50] measured the static and dynamic statement frequencies to determine the relative importance of different constructs. For example, the frequency of procedure call statements were weighted by their cost (in instructions and memory references) and were found to require more resources than any other statement. Ditzel [19] reported the operand use of C language programs in a study of register alternatives. In these two studies the compiler was used to insert data-collecting statements at appropriate points. After program execution, the results were saved for later analysis.

1.1.3: Comparative Analysis

The earliest notable comparative system study by Wichmann [70,71] examined the execution of Algol-60 programs on several different machines. An Algol-60 compiler produced code for a machine called the Whetstone computer [53], a simple stack-oriented machine with a few complex operations to handle variable referencing and parameter passing. The machine was not intended to be built but was used as an intermediate representation of Algol programs that was to be interpreted. This interpretation mechanism allowed very large programs to execute since the address space of the Whetstone could be mapped to backing store.

Wichmann used the interpreter to collect data on the Whetstone instruction stream. The work load represented 155 million instructions and 949 program executions. He then synthesized a small Algol program that had the same Whetstone instruction frequencies as the original work load. For example, the original work load executed the SQRT (square root) instruction 0.17 percent of the time, so the synthetic program used a SQRT instruction the same amount. This synthetic program (termed the *Whetstone benchmark*) was then timed on some fifty machines.

The only measure used by the Wichmann study was time. The results do not allow architectural comparisons but rather measure the complete system: machine, operating system, and compiler. This benchmark program has been used extensively by computer makers, but modern compiler technology makes this synthetic program invalid. The synthetic program duplicates the original work load only at the intermediate Whetstone level. The actual source statements are not derived from the original source programs. To illustrate, the Whetstone frequency of array index operations is duplicated in the synthetic program by array references. The benchmark often uses a constant as the index for these array references, and bears no relation to the actual expressions that the measured programs used as an array index. No longer does the program represent 949 programs; instead it represents a single 100-line program that has no constructive utility. Wichmann warns users of this difficulty, yet the benchmark continues to be misused.

A comprehensive comparative study [25] was performed for the *computer family architecture* (CFA) project. After an extensive process, three architectures (DEC PDP-11, IBM S/370, and Interdata 8/32) were chosen to be analyzed in detail. A model of computer behavior was developed to test statistical hypotheses on three performance measures. The measures reflected the program's static size, memory traffic, and internal register activity. Each measure was modeled to reflect the effect of the programmer, program, architecture, and the many interactions. These effects were estimated from a sample of 16 programmers and 12 assembly language programs. The results showed the 8/32 to be significantly better than the S/370 architecture, but the 8/32 *vs.* PDP-11 and PDP-11 *vs.* S/370 differences were not significant. The instruction streams were measured by the same ISP interpreter used by Lunde [41]. Only the three measures were collected, so specific features of each architecture could not be compared. This book extends the work of the CFA study by making detailed measurements of each architecture in a high-level-language environment.

Other studies have used the benchmarks and measures of the CFA study. Several military computers were compared as an extension of the CFA study [18]. None of the architectures was shown to be significantly better. Stone and Sutherland's study [62] of the VAX 11/780, Z-8000, HP-300, PDP-11, 6701, and 8080 showed significant differences largely due to the basic word size of each machine. A less detailed analysis of the PDP-11, 8086, 68000, and Z-8000 [28] examined program size and speed. In all of these studies the programs are carefully written assembly language routines that do not reflect current use of high-level languages. Differences in the technology used to implement an architecture and the limited measures prevent valid comparisons of the instruction sets.

1.2:   Outline

This book compares architectural features of instruction sets by measuring program execution under an identical work load. The measurements include other effects not reflecting architectural differences; these effects are quantified and factored out of the analysis.

Chapter 2 introduces the mechanisms used to measure high-level-language programs and instruction set execution. A machine-independent representation of a program is explained and its measures are presented. These measures are used as a baseline for later comparative analysis. The emulation laboratory that executed the work load is described, as well as the monitoring system that measured the instruction stream. A more recently developed instruction set simulator called the *Architect's Workbench* is also described.

Chapter 3 presents the results of measuring the four architectures. The work load is characterized and the machine-independent representation is generated. The measurements are divided into three sections: the instruction stream, the memory reference behavior, and the control or branching mechanisms. The instruction stream examines the static size and then focuses on the composition and frequency of instruction components.

Memory referencing results examine the generation of addresses and the types of operands that are fetched or stored. Control instructions are treated apart from the instruction stream because of the importance to machine designers. The analysis looks at the composition of branch instructions and the branch distance behavior.

Chapter 4 examines the variations in the instruction stream due to the compiler. These variations are categorized to identify the source of the effect. Each of these effects is introduced and illustrated. A case study examines the S/370 instruction stream by using six compilers. The compilers range from very simple to quite sophisticated. The analysis is again divided into three sections: the instruction stream, the memory reference behavior, and the control mechanisms. The results are also related to the analysis of Chapter 3.

Chapter 5 is a complement to Chapter 4. By using a single compiler front end, code is generated for several different instruction set architectures. These are synthetic instruction sets—related to S/370, RISC, and stack machines, but normalized to the same ALU operations, etc. This allows the study of various instruction set features such as Register-to-Memory formats, register set sizing, etc. The results can then also be compared to the analysis in Chapter 3.

ANALYZING COMPUTER ARCHITECTURES

Chapter 2

Program and Instruction Set Measurement

Chapter 2: Program and Instruction Set Measurement

Architectural comparisons provide information on which instruction set features are better, but it is also important to know how much of an improvement is possible. This chapter presents the *canonic interpretive* (CI) measures as a set of machine-independent measure of a high-level-language program. The CI measures characterize the static size and dynamic behavior of a program. The measures under certain conditions are a lower bound of the execution demands of a program and are used as a baseline for architectural comparisons.

Both the high-level-language programs and various instruction streams are measured. The language is measured by first determining the CI measures of the program.

Instruction stream measurements can be obtained in many ways. Each mechanism has advantages and disadvantages for particular applications. This study embeds the measurement program, the *monitor*, into the micromachine. An environment to design and implement micromachine-based monitors exists for a universal host, the *Emmy*.

2.1: The CI Measures

The CI measures [21] were developed to assess the size of the smallest representation of a high-level-language program and the minimum work requirements to generate and interpret the program. These measures were used to synthesize architectures [32,67]; applying them to the evaluation of architectures is particularly useful since they are independent of any implementation.

The CI measures are *ideal* (i.e., form a lower bound) under certain (strong) assumptions and constraints. First, there is a one-to-one correspondence between the CI representation and the source. Second, there is no *a priori* knowledge of the frequency distribution of program constructs, neither static nor dynamic. This constraint disallows frequency encoding of variable and operation identifiers in the CI representation. Last, the source is assumed to be in its best form. Any compiler optimization that could improve the representation has already been done on a source-to-source basis.

The CI measures represent five criteria which are used as the basis for comparison throughout this study. They are:

1. *Correspondence*—The CI measure of source correspondence assumes language actions and objects in one-to-one relation with executed instructions and operands. The number of CI operations (instructions) executed is the dynamic number of high-level language actions in the source program.

2. *Size*—The size of each object (in bits) is:

   $\lceil \log_2$ number of similar objects defined in an environment$\rceil$

   Objects are grouped into categories that are semantically distinguishable by the language. Operations, operands, and control transfer points (e.g., labels) are examples of object groups. Environments are bounds on the program region. Typically the region is defined to be a procedure. Operation objects are limited to those found in the procedure and operand objects are restricted to the names available at the current scope.

3. *Activity*—The total number of CI objects accessed is minimized (subject to (1)).

4. *Stability*—The number of environment and control transitions is minimized. The number of procedure entries, computed names (array accesses), and branch actions measure the stability (subject to (1)).

5. *Distance*—The number of unique objects is minimized. This measure pertains to very-high-speed execution and is not used in this study.

The space measure—size—is coupled with the time measures—activity, stability, and distance—to characterize program representations. For example, Table 2.1 shows an augmented listing of a Fortran subroutine. The second column, labeled *Exe*, specifies the number of times the statement was executed. Multiplying the execution count by the CI measure generates the dynamic measures. Table 2.2 summarizes the different CI measures for the entire program from Table 2.1. The next chapter derives the static size measured and uses the CI measures as a baseline for comparisons.

2.2: Instruction Set Measurement

The instruction set of a computer can be measured in many different ways. Measures of the static program representation are simplest to

Table 2.1: Augmented profile with CI measures.

	Exe	Size and Activity			Stability (Branches)		
		Ops	Oprnds	Labels	Enc	Taken	Env
SUBROUTINE CHECK	100						
NM1 = N-1	100	1	3				
DO 10 I=1,NM1	100	1	2				
IF(AKEY(I) .GT. AKEY(I+1))	9900	4	3	1	1	$1-t*$	
FAIL = 1	0	1	2				
10 CONTINUE	9900	1	3	1	1	$1-d*$	
RETURN	100	1			1	1	1
END							

*t represents the fraction of time the statement was true.

*d indicates the fraction of time the associated DO loop was encountered.

Table 2.2: CI measure summary.

Procedure	Size			Activity			Stability (Branches)		
	Ops	Opnds	Labels	Operations	Operands	Labels	Enc	Taken	Env
Main	13	19	5	507	512	500	500	499	0
SETARR.	8	13	5	60,200	110,200	10,000	10,100	10,000	100
SORT	51	89	12	543,512	964,054	166,338	166,438	85,597	100
CHECK	9	13	2	49,800	79,700	19,800	19,900	19,800	100
Totals	81	134	20	654,019	1,154,466	196,638	196,938	115,896	300

CI Measures

Suppose we had data on the execution performance of two different compiler–architecture pairs executing the same benchmark. Or, suppose we had execution data on two different compilers running on the same architecture with the same benchmark. We could conclude the relative merits of one compiler–architecture pair over the other, or one compiler over the other, but we lack an appreciation of just how good the better approach is. We may be comparing a rather mediocre performance to a truly poor performing system.

The canonic interpretive (CI) measures are an attempt to give a measurement baseline to execution performance. The CI measures are derived from the source program. They give the notion of optimality to some parameters, but clearly not a bound. The original source program is simply assumed to be in an optimal form. It may, in fact, be far from it. Source-to-source optimization could reduce a number of the implied statements and operations that would affect the CI measures. The CI measures correspond to an abstract machine that has tight instruction encoding with a robust set of formats to minimize the number of instructions executed during the course of program interpretation, but it is a stack machine (without push or pop overhead). It has limitations: it has no register or primary buffer space to hold values from statement to statement, thus, the CI measure of read and writes may be significantly higher than that realized by actual architectures. Usually the CI static and dynamic instruction counts are better than actual machines. The data read and write traffic, however, tends to be worse than most register set machines. Overall, its value is as an architecture-independent baseline against which both the designer and the compiler writer may compare results.

obtain. The size can sometimes be determined from an existing mechanism such as a compiler or linkage-editor listing. Some compilers produce machine code listings of the program to allow detailed analysis. Static opcode distributions, operand specifiers, branch types, etc., can be determined from these listings. Studies have used such information to frequency encode the instruction set and so minimize program size.

2.2.1: Software and Hardware Monitors

Dynamic measurement mechanisms, that is, devices that measure the sequence of executed instructions, can be divided into three general classes. The first embeds the measuring tool, the monitor, at the same interpretive level as the work load being measured. Termed *software monitors*, they represent a relatively slow-speed but easy-to-build mechanism. Figure 2.1 is taken from Neuhauser [48] to illustrate the location of the monitor relative to the host and image machines. Software monitors are effectively used to analyze instruction measures that require large amounts of storage. For example, instruction pair and triple frequency distributions use storage areas proportional to the square and cube of the number of instructions. The slow speed of the software monitor can change the measurements. For example, the instruction stream will change if certain time constraints are not met while monitoring a low-level disk driver.

Software monitors exist by definition in the same storage mechanisms and use the same interpretive mechanism as the system being monitored. This precludes the ability to study cache and memory performance, since the execution of the monitor affects these parameters. One mechanism used to circumvent this problem relies on statistical sampling of the instruction stream. The monitor is invoked, data collected, and then the execution is continued for some period of time before the monitor is again invoked. These monitor studies can accurately obtain operation code frequencies, average branch distance, etc., but the sequencing information of the instruction stream is lost.

High-level-language program characteristics are efficiently measured by using a specialized type of software monitor. A three-step process is employed that first modifies the original program by inserting statements in each basic block to update a counter array. This program is compiled and executed by using the normal compiler. Once the program completes, the basic block counter array is processed to produce a dynamic profile. The overhead in this method is limited to an array update for each entry to a basic block. Profile generators often exist for several languages as an integral part of the compiler. De Prycker designed a general-purpose system to use a description of the language to be analyzed, a program in that language, and an indication of the desired dynamic statistics. From these descriptions a program that gathers the statistics is produced [51].

A second method for instruction set monitoring builds the collection mechanism into the hardware implementation of the machine. Termed *hardware monitors*, they require an expensive design effort and special intimate access to the machine. Figure 2.2, from Neuhauser, diagrams a typical hardware monitor configuration.

Offsetting the drawbacks, this is an extremely fast and accurate monitor. Cache and memory systems can be analyzed, instruction execution time and other implementation-dependent aspects of an architecture are readily available.

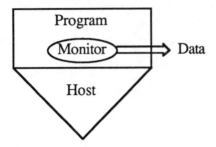

Figure 2.1: Software monitor.

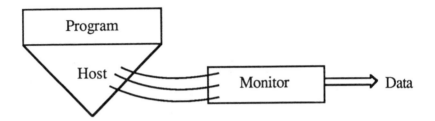

Figure 2.2: Hardware monitor.

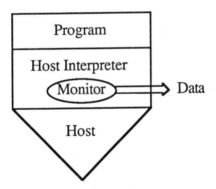

Figure 2.3: Firmware monitor.

Figures 2.1–2.3 are reprinted with permission from *An Emulation Based Analysis of Computer Architecture*, PhD thesis, by C. J. Neuhauser, 1980. Copyright © 1980 by Johns Hopkins University.

CHAPTER 2. MEASUREMENT

The Level Playing Field

It is very difficult to create a fair basis on which to evaluate issues in instruction set architecture. The quality and maturity of a compiler can mask significant architectural deficiencies. Instruction set architectures themselves are the result of complex tradeoffs involving many issues. Even instruction sets that are similar, e.g., register set architectures using the same number of registers, usually differ in multiple other details, making it impossible to determine which of those details gives the advantage to one architecture over another. We believe that the only hope for insight here is in carefully controlled experiments with exhaustive attention to detail on each experiment. This necessitates using a rather small number of benchmarks, thus providing a different kind of limitation. In general it is impossible to find a level playing field in which to measure any and all architectural variations, but it may be possible to find regions in which a fair comparison can be performed. These regions become all the more important as the field of computer architecture advances.

Another important advantage of hardware monitors is the ability to measure complete systems without degrading their performance. Paging and cache studies are accurately performed and alternate designs can often be analyzed. A study of the VAX architecture [16] evaluated different address translation buffer sizes by using a hardware monitor.

2.2.2: *Firmware Monitors*

An intermediate monitoring mechanism embeds the data collection program into the interpretive mechanism. In this case the interpretive mechanism must itself be a machine. *Firmware monitors* combine many of the advantages of software and firmware monitors without the drawbacks. Figure 2.3, from Neuhauser, shows the location of such a mechanism. A firmware monitor is programmed in the same language as the emulator for the image machine, and has access to all aspects of the instruction execution. This includes intermediate states during instruction interpretation, potentially a storage area outside that defined for the image machine, and the ability to scale and schedule external events to model different hardware configurations.

Firmware monitors are used to collect data for three architectures used in this study. A software monitor is used for a fourth architecture (VAX), as an emulator for this architecture does not yet exist. A measurement environment is described, as well as the monitors designed to execute within this system.

The Stanford Emulation Laboratory has served many roles, but as far as this work is concerned its primary role was that of a firmware monitoring facility. The heart of the facility was a universal host—a machine designed to interpret a wide range of image instruction sets—which was used as an experimental testbed for comparative analysis. The machine, *Emmy*, was an outgrowth of a series of hardware studies based upon processor designs with fast memories. While viewed as being a special-purpose processor, designed primarily for interpretation, its organization resembled many of the modern RISC machines perhaps because of a common concern with the interpretation process (such as running operating systems or emulators) and with design targeted to high-speed-memory components.

Some of Emmy's features included:

1. A fixed 32-bit instruction.

2. A load–store type of instruction set, two instruction fragments in each instruction word: one for register-based ALU operations, the other for load or store activities.

3. A branch instruction that can be substituted in either fragment. Moreover, Emmy included excellent support for field extraction as required in emulation.

The primary difference between Emmy and a more modern RISC processor would be Emmy's limited high speed storage (16K bytes), which serves as an explicit cache. The Emmy prototype, based upon design studies performed earlier, was built at Palyn Associates in San Jose and installed at Stanford in 1974. Early emulation efforts were restricted to processor emulation only and the development of software tools to support such emulation. By the late 1970's, UNIX was adopted as the basic method of I/O emulation. Thereafter, both I/O and processor architectures were emulated. Emmy as an experimental tool was unique to Stanford. However, the Emmy processor had a production version produced by ICL called the ME-29. This machine was distributed widely throughout Europe to support interpretation of various ICL architectures.

The Emulation Laboratory is organized as shown in Figure 2.4. The processor has writable control store (4K × 32 bits) to support both emulation and performance monitoring [47]. The memory system is designed to be configured by the emulator to closely match the needs of the image machine [46]. A bus adaptor connects the Emmy system to a UNIX system that provides complete device emulation, console support, debugging, and program development [34,35,58].

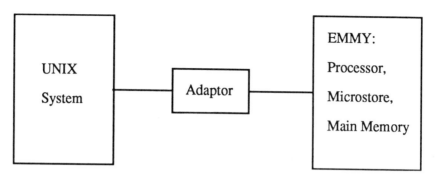

Figure 2.4: The Emulation Laboratory.

The emulators used in the Emulation Laboratory, with the monitor turned on, execute around 20 thousand instructions per second. This reflects a slowdown by a factor of 2 or 3 over the normal emulator. The VAX software monitor proceeds at only 120–180 instructions per second; a more than two order of magnitude difference. The VAX monitor was carefully used so that it would not be necessary to run the test programs a second time.

Monitor Design and Implementation

An emulator interprets image instructions by mimicking the actions of the real machine. Machine cycles such as *fetch*, *decode*, etc., map to equivalent microcoded procedures. A firmware monitor can be coded directly into these routines or may exist as a separate module called at a specific point during the interpretation. Often a combination of these methods is used.

The PDP-11 firmware monitor distributes the collection of information throughout the emulator, but updates the counters at the end of an image instruction [48]. The S/370 and P-code monitors have a separate information collection module called at the beginning of an image instruction. This may replicate some of the interpretation, but it is easier to use with existing emulators. In some instructions it is necessary to replace a normal execution cycle routine with one instrumented to collect data. This is used for instructions for which performance measures depend on execution. For example, the S/370 LOAD instruction always loads a 4-byte object from main memory, but the EDIT instruction references a byte stream whose size depends on the data itself.

The function of a monitor is to record events. The mechanism employed depends on different constraints. An early monitoring mechanism used trace tapes to hold a record of events for later analysis. Trace tapes not only explicitly record an event, but implicitly record the sequence of events. The major drawback of traces is the large volume of data generated for a very short period of time. An address trace of a large IBM machine could fill a 2400 foot tape in less than a second. One solution to this problem is to combine the data collection monitor and the analysis program into a single module. A firmware monitor is well suited for this situation. For example, an architectural measure such as the distribution of instruction lengths can be calculated from a trace tape with a single pass through the data. On the other hand, a firmware monitor can update a small set of counters as each instruction is executed. After the work load is completed, the array of counters gives the desired distribution, but no tape is required. In this example, a counter records the event and the sequence of the events is lost.

Events are grouped into one of three categories. A *simple* event is a time-invariant occurrence, such as the execution of a branch-on-condition instruction. Simple events are often stored as counters, and answer questions such as "how frequent?" "what average?" and "how many?". They do not depend on past execution. A *time-stamp* event records the time an event occurred. The unit of time depends on the needs for other events that depend on it. The monitors in this study record time in the number of instructions executed. For example, the run length is the number of sequentially executed instructions until a branch. A time-stamp event records the time (in instructions) of every taken branch, so the distance from the last branch is easily calculated.

The last event type, *sequential events*, is a function of simple and time-stamp events. The run length of the last example is calculated as the difference between a simple event, (e.g., a taken branch) and a time-stamp event (e.g., the last taken branch). Consider the S/370 branch instruction; it can be conditional or unconditional, and the target address is calculated by adding an optional base and index register to a displacement. A measure important to pipelined machines is "how far back in the instruction stream could the outcome and location of this branch be resolved?". The S/370 monitor records the time each register is modified and the time the condition codes are updated. The resolution time is calculated as the time of the most recent change to the register and condition codes used by the instruction.

The monitors in this study record events of interest to instruction set design. The instruction operation, opcode, is first determined. The operand specifications are then extracted and appropriate counters are updated. A two-dimensional counter array is used by the PDP-11 for operand counters. The first index is the operation and the second is the operand specification. The S/370 and P-code architectures have a much simpler operand specification, and the monitors need fewer counters. The VAX monitor is organized differently. The operand specifier is stored not as a function of the instruction but as a function of the access and data type. For example, one group of counters is used for all instructions which read a 4-byte integer and another group for floating-point writes. The method is used because of the large number of operation, operand pairs that exist.

Event counters are maintained by the emulator and are then available for analysis. These counters provide the values necessary to calculate opcode distributions and instruction class distributions (number of adds, branches, etc.). Operand counters generate memory and register reference distributions. In the P-code architecture, operand specifiers for the stack are implicit and must be inferred from the opcode distribution. The calculation of some architectural measures can be quite complicated, requiring the scaling and summing of many different counters.

A final function of a monitor is to limit the address range of instructions being analyzed. As shown later, comparative analysis requires precise control of this range. The firmware monitors are designed to compare the current instruction's address to first determine if it is within the range to be monitored. This bounding of the monitor's range is an important tool that allows fair architectural comparisons.

The Evolution of the Emulation Laboratory

The degree of fidelity becomes an important issue in the design of an emulator, since the difficulty of producing an accurate duplication of all actions of a target architecture can become a formidable and time-consuming task. To clarify this issue, classes of emulation have been defined.

Class A emulators duplicate the action of a target architecture in all respects so that the emulator can pass the so-called Turing test. Even "illegal" code sequences in the emulated machine fail in the same way as they would in a true target implementation. The emulator machine and the target machine are, from a logical point of view, indistinguishable implementations; only execution times differ.

For class B emulation, the action of correct programs is properly duplicated. Incorrect code sequences may cause unpredictable differences between the emulated result and the true target result. In the commercial arena, a plug-compatible machine, or PCM supplier, is required to provide a class A emulation of an architecture which is to be emulated. Otherwise diagnostic and debugging support and other tools will not properly operate.

Class C emulation is a class B emulation that does not fully support all correct programs. Thus, certain infrequently used instruction types may be missing, or the data types might use a representation slightly different from the target architecture.

Class D is anything else. Lower classes of emulation are possible, and in fact could prove very valuable. While not producing an exact duplicate action in the emulator as in the target architecture, they can be used to ensure that a similar number of identifiable actions are produced in an emulated architecture as in the target architecture. The statistical similarity can then be used to evaluate the overall architectural performance of the target architecture.

Most of the early emulation efforts were class B. The results described in Chapters 3 and 4 of this book are based on either class B emulation or on direct measurement of a target machine.

As studies and analysis progressed in the laboratory, it became clear that class B emulation and the fidelity it represented to a target architecture was not required for successful architectural evaluation. Indeed, by forcing the use of actual disparate compilers, additional sources of non-architectural issues were introduced (as we shall see in later chapters) and it became clear that other techniques would be more useful for architectural evaluation.

After a series of design exercises, it was determined that a much (10–50 times) more powerful version of Emmy could be realized simply based upon better technology or more ambitious implementation. However, since class A or B emulation appeared no longer to be a pressing requirement, other alternatives for architectural evaluation were explored and adopted. This lead to the development of the Architect's Workbench, a software simulation platform for architectural evaluation described in the next section. The move to the architect's workbench approach is based upon the following considerations.

1. The almost universal availability of powerful computational workstations.

2. The development of software techniques that do not require the traditional instruction-by-instruction emulation for the evaluation of any architecture.

3. The need to perform an approximate architectural evaluation early in the evolution of a target architecture. Approximate architecture descriptions must be evaluated on existing applications. The more traditional approach has high-fidelity architecture descriptions evaluated on small kernels of software.

With the successful completion of the Architect's Workbench in 1984–1985, the Emmy processor was decommissioned in 1986.

The Architect's Workbench

In the evaluation of an instruction set architecture, the typical approach is to do a complete design at the register transfer level, and then implement/simulate this design by using small test programs (kernels) as input. Indeed, for a new design, since the software (compiler, etc.) has not yet been completed, these small test kernels form the universe of discussion and evaluation for architectural decisions. We have low fidelity software on top of a high fidelity hardware model.

The Architect's Workbench is an attempt to turn this around to allow complete applications (program test suites), which are somehow representative of the target application environment to run on approximations to the hardware instruction set. The AWB assumes an ALU vocabulary consistent with that used in the high-level language. The user then specifies the number of parameters which determine basic instruction encoding, number of registers available for various functions, etc.—just enough information to determine the dynamic program behavior for the instruction and data stream. This, then, allows cache evaluation and basic tradeoffs in architecture, now with real software driving an approximate description of the hardware.

2.3:   The Architect's Workbench

The Architect's Workbench [40] was developed as a very-high-level simulator to support research in computer architecture. The simulator has a repertoire of more than fifty recognizable architectures with many other variations possible by parameter specification. The simulator is particularly useful to designers doing initial tradeoff among high-level design constructs, such as cache, register set size, register allocation policy, etc.

The simulator is outlined in Figure 2.5. An application in one of several acceptable high-level languages is compiled into a standard intermediate form, and its execution is then simulated by using an architecture/cache simulator. The simulator input of the architecture is a very-high-level description—a series of parameters describing a particular architecture. Currently the AWB accepts applications written in Pascal, Fortran, or C, and supports three architectural families, including:

1. Stack, which includes P-code (simple stack), byte-encoded stack, and B6700 type architectures.

2. Register set architectures, including RISC (a load–store architecture with fixed 32-bit instructions) and IBM 360 type architectures.

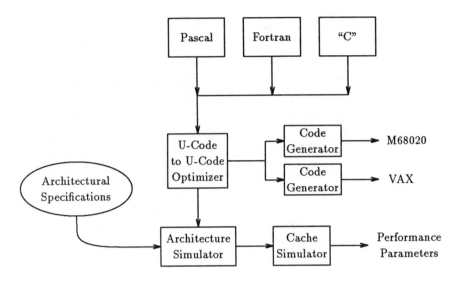

Figure 2.5: Architect's Workbench system.

3. Direct Correspondence Architectures (an approximate realization of the canonic interpretive measures) [68].

2.3.1: Basic Operation

Applications written in higher level languages are translated into a standard intermediate form. This form is broken into basic blocks—groups of instructions that are always executed together. The application is then executed interpretively on a host machine by using the intermediate form. The result is a basic block trace of the program execution, which generates a table of basic block usage.

Based upon the architectural specifications for a particular architecture under study, code is later generated for each of the basic blocks in the table. Performance predictions can be made for the execution of the program based upon the result of this code generation, since the performance characteristic of each basic block and the number of times that basic block has been executed are now known.

2.3.2: Using the AWB

It is possible to make basic architectural tradeoffs among several primary and numerous secondary architectural parameters (Figure 2.6).

A primary tradeoff is between the instruction bandwidth (dynamic count of instruction bits required to execute a program) and the complexity of the instruction decoder. Clearly, a more complex instruction

CHAPTER 2. MEASUREMENT

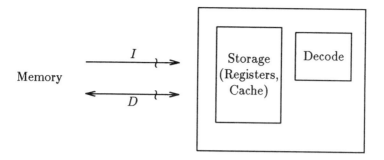

Figure 2.6: Basic tradeoff between memory bandwidth (I and D), internal processor storage (S), and processor decode requirements.

set requires fewer bits from memory to represent the program during execution. If an instruction cache is used, the size of the cache varies with the amount of instruction encoding for a fixed memory bandwidth from memory.

The allocation of data storage within a processor can be studied by varying the number of registers to understand their effect on data bandwidth. If a data cache is present and the data bandwidth is held constant, one can optimize the allocation of resources to registers and to data cache. E.g., for an area limited microprocessor, the effectiveness of allocation of additional area to registers diminishes after a number of registers are implemented; thereafter, area should be allocated to data cache.

Finally, many issues in the specification of a cache may be studied, such as replacement policy, the block or line size, etc., to determine the best overall strategy to enhance architectural performance.

2.3.3: *The User's View of the Architect's Workbench*

The AWB is designed to provide easy access to multiple architectures and multiple cache organizations, by allowing rapid high-level simulation. In general the user needs to specify only about a dozen parameters to define a processor model. Alternatively, the user may simply call a prespecified processor model already defined in the AWB vocabulary. In order to achieve such simplicity of use, the AWB uses a number of default conventions. In particular, the initial ALU or arithmetic or functional vocabulary is assumed to be defined by the high-level language. Data path widths are also covered by default convention (one word wide), and I/O issues are usually ignored. Despite these approximations, the AWB description for architectures such as S/360, P-code, and RISC generally are accurate to within 10 percent, assuming a comparable level of compiler optimization.

As a high-level simulator, the AWB is complementary to other system level tools such as ISPS [8]. The ISP type simulators are behavioral simulators; the user provides a register transfer description of the processor. This requires a complete instruction-level definition of the processor. As such, the AWB can be a front end to behavioral simulators such as ISP. After initial high-level tradeoffs have been completed by using the AWB, the user completes the processor description and continues further simulation and tradeoff studies on a more detailed level by using register transfer type simulation.

2.3.4: The Architectures

Tables 2.3 and 2.4 illustrate some of the parameters available for specifying either a member of the register set architecture family (Table 2.3) or a member of the stack family (Table 2.4). The user either calls one of the prespecified architectures with its parameter set, or specifies a more appropriate set of parameters for the architecture under consideration. The benchmark under analysis is translated into a common intermediate form called U-code [49]. U-code is similar in many ways to P-code, an intermediate form for Pascal programs. The Architect's Workbench currently supports translation from Fortran, Pascal, and C into U-code. The U-code version of the application is then arranged into basic blocks. A basic block is a sequence of instructions with a single entry and a single exit point. If the first instruction in a basic block is executed, then all instructions in the basic block are executed. Each instruction, of course, is a basic block. The system constructs maximum size basic blocks by combining instructions that always sequentially follow each other in execution. Basic block analysis is used [4] to reduce the complexity of tracing. The execution of the U-code is interpreted once and a count of the number of times each basic block is executed is retained in the basic block trace of the program, thus creating a basic block data file. This data file contains the basic block numbers, sizes, and starting positions in U-code. The architectural specifications allow code to be generated for each basic block according to the parameters indicated. This allows an estimation of basic block size for the actual architecture specified.

After the basic block analysis is completed, cache simulation is performed by using a pseudo-execution of the program. When a benchmark begins cache simulation, it executes a call initialization routine

Table 2.3: Parameters specified for register set architectures and sample architectures.

Architecture	o	a	c	m	b	r	l	e	p	s	w
regdef	8	8	24	24	24	1	0	N	1	N	N
hp	16	1	0	8	4	1	0	N	1	N	N
OBI360-1	16	16	0	16	16	1	0	N	1	N	N
OBI360-2	16	16	0	16	16	2	0	N	1	N	N
OBI360-3	16	16	0	16	16	3	0	N	1	N	N
OBI360-4	16	16	0	16	16	4	0	N	1	N	N
OBI360-5	16	16	0	16	16	5	0	N	1	N	N
OBI360l-1	16	16	0	16	16	5	1	N	1	N	N
OBI360l-2	16	16	0	16	16	5	2	N	1	N	N
OBI360l-3	16	16	0	16	16	5	3	N	1	N	N
OBI360l-4	16	16	0	16	16	5	4	N	1	N	N
OBI360l-5	16	16	0	16	16	5	5	N	1	N	N
OBI360o-1	16	16	0	16	16	5	1	Y	1	N	N
OBI360o-2	16	16	0	16	16	5	2	Y	1	N	N
OBI360o-3	16	16	0	16	16	5	3	Y	1	N	N
OBI360o-4	16	16	0	16	16	5	4	Y	1	N	N
OBI360o-5	16	16	0	16	16	5	5	Y	1	N	N
OBI360o-6	16	16	0	16	16	5	6	Y	1	N	N
OBI360o-7	16	16	0	16	16	5	7	Y	1	N	N
OBI360o-8	16	16	0	16	16	5	8	Y	1	N	N
OBI360o-9	16	16	0	16	16	5	9	Y	1	N	N
Fix32-0	32	32	0	0	0	7	0	Y	0	N	N
Fix32-1	32	32	0	0	0	7	1	Y	0	N	N
Fix32-2	32	32	0	0	0	7	2	Y	0	N	N
Fix32-3	32	32	0	0	0	7	3	Y	0	N	N
Fix32-4	32	32	0	0	0	7	4	Y	0	N	N
Fix32-5	32	32	0	0	0	7	5	Y	0	N	N
Fix32-6	32	32	0	0	0	7	6	Y	0	N	N
Fix32-7	32	32	0	0	0	7	7	Y	0	N	N
Fix32-8	32	32	0	0	0	7	8	Y	0	N	N
Fix32-9	32	32	0	0	0	7	9	Y	0	N	N
Fix32-m	32	32	0	0	0	7	9	Y	1	N	N
B-mmm	8	8	8	24	24	5	5	Y	2	Y	N
B-mmr	8	8	8	24	24	5	5	Y	2	N	N
B-rmr	8	8	8	24	24	5	5	Y	1	N	N
B-rrr	8	8	8	24	24	5	5	Y	0	N	N
OBI360o-w	16	16	0	16	16	5	15	Y	1	N	Y
Fix32-w	32	32	0	0	0	7	15	Y	1	N	Y

o: bits for simple RR opcode
a: alignment of branch targets
c: additional bits for small constant
m: additional bits for each memory reference
b: bits additional for each branch target

r: registers available for temporaries
l: registers available for local variables
e: Use exact register allocation?
p: number of operand sources allowed (0,1,2)
s: Op destination allowed in memory?
w: Special register window simulation?

Table 2.4: Parameters specified for stack architectures and resulting sample architectures.

Architecture	o	a	c	r	b
P-code	32	32	32	32	N
Stack	8	8	16	32	N
Stack816a	8	32	16	32	N
S816a64	8	64	16	32	N
S816a128	8	128	16	32	N
b6700	8	8	X	16	Y
b6700a	8	32	X	16	Y

o: bits for simple opcode
a: alignment of branch targets
c: bits for instruction with small constant
r: bits for instruction with memory reference
b: special changes for B6700

that reads the basic block table and modifies it so that it represents the memory addresses and lengths corresponding to the architecture being studied. The simulation of program execution through the cache resembles the activity required to manage a cache table.

Overall the AWB has proven to be quite effective, by allowing rapid estimation of performance of various architectures once a single program interpretation has been done.

2.3.5: Status

The Architect's Workbench is currently used for architectural research and runs under UNIX. It is being extended to improve the design environment for application specific integrated circuit (ASIC) microprocessors.

2.4: Issues in Architecture

The purpose of this book is to quantitatively examine the effects that processor architectures have on important performance parameters. The machines or architectures studied include:

1. IBM S/370. Now more than 25 years old, this architecture has been a dominant processor design in the mainframe area and has heavily influenced generations of machine designers.

2. Digital Equipment Corporation's VAX architecture. This has become a pervasive machine line in the intermediate engineering and scientific marketplace.

3. Hewlett–Packard's Precision Architecture. This is not as well known as the preceding architectures. It is a RISC (reduced instruction set computer) architecture (a load–store architecture with fixed 32-bit instruction size). The Precision Architecture has been chosen as being representative of the RISC approach. Its instruction set is probably better encoded than many other RISC architectures.

4. P-code. P-code was originally developed as an intermediate form for Pascal. It represents a simple stack machine with fixed 32-bit size instructions.

5. Ideal machine. The canonic form discussed in the next chapter represents an idealized instruction set. The CI measures referred to in Chapters 3 and 4 represent parametric minima or expected values based upon source language considerations only.

CI-based machines have been an important study area at Stanford and there have been various architectures designed and emulated that come close to achieving or bettering the CI measures. The DELtran architecture was developed for Fortran [33] and the Adept architecture for Pascal [67]. The DCA described in Chapter 5 is basically identical to Adept and is a close approximation to CI measures for Pascal for the program set described in that chapter.

As we shall see, compilation is a major factor in architectural performance. If the compiler strategy is not a carefully controlled variable, the resulting architectural evaluations are of little value and may indeed give quite erroneous or deceptive indications. Chapter 4 discusses the effects of various compiler strategies on a single architecture, S/370. In Chapter 3, a comparative evaluation of the above architectures is presented for two compiler strategies: a middle-ground strategy corresponding to medium optimization, or optimization level 1 in IBM terms, and an optimized level.

In Chapter 5, the compiler is held invariant and the code generator is changed to allow the generation of code that approximates each of the architectures mentioned above. The results of Chapter 5 are compared with results and ratios determined in Chapter 3.

The benchmarks or test set used in Chapters 3 and 4 are also used in Chapter 5. Additional benchmarks are included in Chapter 5 to better measure the effect of cache size and dynamic program size. Several of the programs used in Chapters 3 and 4 have a small stack size and are limited in the context of the Chapter 5 study.

ANALYZING COMPUTER ARCHITECTURES

Chapter 3

Comparative Data

Chapter 3: Comparative Data

This chapter describes the environment for this study and examines the static and dynamic characteristics of different programs executing on a diverse range of instruction set architectures. The environment includes the test set of programs, the instruction set architectures on which they execute, and the compilers used to translate the programs.

The test set of programs, or work load, is first characterized by examining the static and dynamic distribution of high-level-language constructs. These results are compared with other studies to verify the scientific orientation of the work load.

The data generated by the representation and execution of the test set cover many areas of instruction set analysis. Static program measures reflect the efficiency of the instruction set's encoding. This measure is sensitive to the address width. The 16-bit PDP-11 produces the smallest representation, but the machine designed as an address extension of the PDP-11, the VAX, produces a much larger representation. The size of the CI representation is many times smaller than the architectures used in this study.

Dynamic analysis provides many important measures of instruction set effectiveness. The CI model is used as a baseline for comparison to determine not only the relative effectiveness of an architecture, but also the extent of possible improvement.

After the beginning section on the environment, this chapter's analysis is divided into three separate sections. The first section examines the dynamic and static characteristics of the instruction stream. The second section focuses on the memory reference behavior. This behavior is related to the high-level-language variable access profiles. The final section analyzes the branch mechanisms used in each architecture.

3.1:   The Environment

A program's environment includes only a portion of the period of a machine's execution. For an interactive computer system this execution period might begin after an initial carriage return is typed, and continues until a prompt signals the completion of the program. In this case, the machine not only executes the program but also schedules

Table 3.1: Overhead memory references (in bytes).

Program	Machine		
	IBM S/370	VAX 11/780	P-Code
FFT	130 Thousand	222 Thousand	171 Thousand
Mort	1.5 Million	25 Million	4.96 Million
Norm	822 Thousand	5.3 Million	2.78 Million

other programs, services interrupts, swaps tasks, formats and initiates input/output, and potentially many more activities. To fairly compare architectures on some test set of programs, the period of machine execution that is measured must be restricted. It would be unfair to make architectural judgments on machine code size if the entire run-time library is included. For this study, only those instructions generated by a compiler for a particular program are included. The programs in the test set were initially written in Fortran. This source was used as a basis when the programs were translated to other languages. Any extra code needed to support Fortran run-time environments is excluded from the analysis. For example, the Fortran built-in function DMAX1 was written in the Pascal version of one test program, and its execution was excluded from the analysis. In a similar fashion, I/O was excluded. There is a great deal of variability in the I/O support offered by the machines in this study. For the IBM S/370 the operating system often organizes files in fixed blocks, while UNIX uses variable-length lines of text. Table 3.1 shows the number of memory references (in bytes) as the result of overhead instructions. The variability of these data reflects the different environments and levels of support offered by each operating system. It is interesting to note that the oldest and most carefully optimized I/O environment of the S/370 machine is the most effective.

3.1.1: The Architectures

Five instruction set architectures were selected for this study. Three of the machines were supported through emulators available in the Stanford Emulation Laboratory. The other two architectures were monitored by using a software monitor (an instruction tracing facility); one machine (VAX) was also monitored by using a firmware monitor.

The IBM S/360 and S/370 machines were initially designed in the early 1960s and represent a memory/register architecture [6]. Small, upward compatible extensions to the S/360 produced the S/370. The initial S/360 emulator [69] was extended to include single and double precision floating point and a select set of the S/370 architecture extensions used by the S/370 high-level-language compilers are provided to allow execution of the unaltered object files produced by the S/370 Fortran and Pascal compilers. The emulator provides necessary support for OS system calls.

The DEC PDP-11 processor represents a typical vintage 16-bit microprogrammed machine, and combines many features of stack and register machines. The emulator for the PDP-11 supports the basic architecture and includes several I/O device emulations [45]. This emulator can run the same operating system (Mini-UNIX) that is used on a PDP-11 in the Emmy lab. The Mini-UNIX operating system supports the high-level-language C. Other language compilers have been produced for UNIX but are generally unavailable for Mini-UNIX. The floating-point and extended instruction set of the PDP-11 architecture is not supported by the emulator but is used by the C compiler. The operating system is designed to trap instructions not supported by the hardware and interpret them in software. With this mechanism, low-cost machines without floating-point hardware can execute floating-point programs with no modification to the compiler. Therefore, by carefully selecting the time that the instruction set is monitored, the resulting statistics indicate how a full implementation of the architecture would have executed.

A stack-oriented machine, the P-code pseudo-machine is an architecture designed to transport a Pascal compiler to different host computers. Although not intended to be a commercial architecture, many interpreters for the machine have been designed. The P-code emulator on the Emmy processor includes I/O and floating-point functions [5]. The P-code compiler is executed on the P-code machine as a production program. The machine code generated by the compiler is not optimized in any way. Interesting statistics about high-level-language programs can be deduced, since many high-level-language constructs often map directly to P-code instructions. For example, the Call Standard Procedure (CSP) instruction indicates the frequency and type of I/O needed by the program. Also the CSP instruction counts trigonometric functions used by a program. For most other machines, it is necessary to examine the number of times the math library was called to determine similar statistics.

At the user level, the VAX architecture is largely an address and data type extension of the PDP-11 architecture. It includes several new functions designed to increase the performance of high-level-language execution. An emulator for the VAX does not exist, and CI measures for the VAX were obtained by executing programs on an actual VAX machine by using a software monitor.

The Hewlett–Packard Precision Architecture [9,31,42] (earlier known as the HP Spectrum) may be regarded as a second-generation RISC, or reduced instruction set, machine. It has a fixed instruction size of 32 bits and uses a load–store instruction format—all ALU operations must reside in registers, and memory references are only used with a load or store from or to registers. It has 32 general purpose registers. The HP-PA represents an improvement in instruction encoding over earlier RISC approaches in that often two—even independent—actions may be specified in a single instruction. Thus, the compare-and-branch and move-and-branch operations can be executed as single instructions.

3.1.2: The Program Test Set

The programs used in Chapters 3 and 4 represent a mix of general purpose scientific computing. Two of the programs are short (around 100 Pascal source lines), and two are longer (around 1300 Pascal source lines).

Fast fourier transform (FFT): Generates a pseudo-random 256 point complex vector, performs a complex FFT and then transforms the data again to restore the original vector as a check. Selected values are printed to verify the execution of the program. The program is characterized as a floating-point numerical program with deterministic control flow. Control structures whose flow can be determined at compile time or at procedure entry time are termed *deterministic control structures*. For example, the **repeat** loops that comprise the core of the FFT program could be completely rolled out once the length of the transform is known.

Sort: Generates a pseudo-random 100 element integer vector, sorts the vector by using a non-recursive quicksort algorithm, and checks the sorted vector (repeated 100 times). Sort is an integer program with both determinate and data-driven control structures. The procedures that fill and check the vector use deterministic control while the sort routine itself uses control structures whose execution depends on the data. As the majority of execution time is spent sorting the data, the program mostly executes data-driven control structures. As Sort is used as an example in several sections of this book, a complete listing of this program is found in Appendix A.

Mort: Converts a program written in Mortran, a structured extension to the Fortran language, into a standard program. Mort is characterized as a character processing program with data-driven control. The program is written in Mortran and characters are stored as integers since Fortran does not support character data types. The program is written to be independent of the character set and often must use sequential searches to locate items.

Norm: Integrates a system of 21 first-order ordinary differential equations by using an adaptive technique. Norm is characterized as a floating-point numerical program with a mix of deterministic and data-driven control structures. In this program the control flow is conditional on floating-point results.

The test programs were all originally written in Fortran and reflect the semantics of that language. The Fortran versions were used on S/370, VAX, and HP-PA. Each program was translated to the languages C and Pascal to be executed on the PDP-11 and P-code architectures. As discussed later, a different Pascal-based test program suite was also included for the Chapter 5 evaluation. Results from both suites are compared in that chapter.

The static distribution of statement types is shown in Table 3.2. Table 3.3 compares similar distributions for several studies. The test programs used a greater than average number of assignment and **goto** statements. Procedure call percentages reported by the other studies do not indicate whether functions, predefined functions, or predefined procedure calls are included. This study used **if** statements with the same frequency, but used fewer loop constructs.

The dynamic distribution of high-level-language statements for the test programs was determined by profiling the execution of the Pascal versions. The Pascal versions kept the same logical structure as the original Fortran, but logical **if–goto** statement pairs were replaced (when possible) by **if-then-else** structures and occasionally by loop structures. The number of conditional and unconditional control decisions and the reference patterns of the variables were carefully preserved. The static statement distributions for the Pascal versions are very similar to the Fortran distribution with fewer **goto** statements and a proportional increase in the **if** and **for** statement types. Table 3.4 shows the distribution of executed statement constructs. The column labeled *This Study* is the average for the test set. The last row, labeled *Other*, indicates the percentage not specified by that study. Compared to the few other studies of dynamic high-level-language execution, the test set executed more assignment statements and far fewer procedure call statements. The programs analyzed in Patterson [50] and Tanenbaum [66] are system-oriented programs (e.g., compilers, file compare, macro expansion) while the programs in this study are scientifically oriented. The seemingly low loop frequency results from counting only the entry of the loop rather than each iteration.

Table 3.2: Static statement distribution.

	FFT	Mort	Norm	Sort	Average
Assignment	56.6	39.9	61.1	52.3	52.5
If	7.5	23.5	12.0	20.0	15.8
Goto	7.5	29.5	9.9	18.5	16.4
Procedure or Function Call*	18.9	6.4	9.7	4.6	9.9
Loop	9.4	.7	7.2	4.6	5.5

*Includes built-in functions.

Table 3.3: Static statement distribution survey.

	Knuth	Robinson	Tanenbaum	Wortman	Alexander	Elshoff	Sweet
Work Load	Scientific	Scientific	System	Student	System	Commercial	System
Language	Fortran	Fortran	SAL	Student/PL	XPL	PL/I	Mesa
Assign	41	36.1	46.5	63.9	42	49.2	28.9
If	14.5	12.5	17.2	10	13	21.3	9.2
Goto	13.0	9.8	—	.3	1	14.0	.5
Call	8	3.2	24.6	2.7	13	3.7	33.8
Loop	4	3.9	5.0	14.8	14	8.6	2.5
Other	19.5	34.5	6.7	8.3	17	3.2	25.1

Table 3.4: Dynamic statement distribution survey.

	This Study	Knuth	Patterson		Tanenbaum
Language	Pascal	Fortran	Pascal	C	SAL
Work Load	Scientific	Student	System	System	System
Assign	74	67	45	38	42
Loop	4	3	5	3	4
Call	1	3	15	12	12
If	20	11	29	43	36
Goto	2	9	–	3	–
Other	–	7	6	1	6

Table 3.5: Dynamic reference percentages (by type).

	FFT	Mort	Norm	Sort	Average
Int	48.5	73.3	53.9	73.4	62.3
Real	24.2	–	9.2	–	8.4
Array	27.3	26.7	33.3	17.2	26.1
Boolean	–	–	.1	–	–
Record	–	–	3.5	9.4	3.2

The static and dynamic statement distributions give an excellent characterization of the test set used in this study. The variable reference patterns for these programs were also obtained for the Pascal versions. Table 3.5 lists the dynamic reference behavior for each program. The array and record entries duplicate counts with the base type of the structure. For example, an integer array reference updates both the *Int* and *Array* rows.

Another way to examine reference behavior is to categorize references by their use. Table 3.6 summarizes variable use for the test set. Since each program was first written in Fortran, the Pascal translations reflect this fact with the almost exclusive use of reference parameters. Value parameters are only used in the translations when a constant is passed.

This examination of the test programs provides a useful characterization of the work load. There are few comparable studies of dynamic program behavior. The results of a study by Patterson [50] of the reference frequency (by use) for a set of Pascal programs is shown in Table 3.7. Compared with Table 3.6 the Fortran-based programs reference more locals and parameters passed by reference (RefParms), and fewer parameters passed by value (ValParms). The *Other* category includes heap references and pointer de-referencing.

Table 3.6: Percent dynamic reference distribution (by use).

	FFT	Mort	Norm	Sort	Average
Local	60.8	.6	62.9	74.8	49.8
Global	2.4	99.0	7.8	7.7	29.2
RefParm	36.0	.2	29.4	17.5	20.8
ValParm	.7	.3	–	–	.2

Table 3.7: Percent dynamic reference distribution (by use) from Patterson [50].

	Program					Average
	Ack	Compare	Macro	Compile	Pretty	
Local	45	31	34	22	29	32
Global	2	31	53	63	25	35
RefParm	–	18	2	1	26	9
ValParm	53	–	8	9	5	15
Other	–	20	3	5	16	9

3.1.3: Compilers

Our comparative evaluation is based on two compiler strategies: simple and optimized. Many compilers exist for the different machines in this study. The IBM S/370 series of computers has three compilers available; Fortran G, Fortran H, and Pascal/VS. The Fortran H compiler [57] provides four levels of optimization. This results in six different representations on the S/370 architecture. These compilers represent a range of compiler organization and optimizations from poor to the very best. The Fortran H optimization level 1 (abbreviated Hopt1) is most representative of a medium-quality compiler available for the other machines used in this study. We designate this medium-quality compiler strategy a *simple compiler*, and we designate Fortran H level 3 as an *optimized compiler*.

The DEC PDP-11 emulator supports the Mini-UNIX operating system and provides a C language compiler [38]. This compiler used an optimization pass to eliminate branch chains and redundant register loads. No implicit register allocation is performed and it relies heavily on the programmer to explicitly allocate often-used variables to registers. The code produced makes effective use of the memory-to-memory operations allowed by the architecture. There were no attempts to program the C translations to use pointer or register variables. Therefore, the statistics for the PDP-11 measure a memory-to-memory architecture. Registers are used only for address calculation and intermediate values. While this restriction does not allow direct comparisons of the PDP-11 to an S/370 machine, it allows a comparison between a load/store register architecture and a memory-to-memory architecture. The Pascal compiler for the P-code machine is a simple non-optimizing compiler. The stack architecture allows little optimization, and the statistics therefore indicate quite closely the performance of this class of architecture.

Finally, the portable C compiler available for the VAX UNIX operating system was targeted to Fortran 77. This is quite similar to the PDP-11 C compiler and again restricts comparisons to those aspects of the VAX architecture used by the compiler, namely memory-to-memory operations and powerful addressing modes.

The VAX VMS compiler represents optimized Fortran and corresponds reasonably well to the complexity contained in IBM's compiler H level 3. The HP Precision Architecture (HP-PA) had only an optimized Fortran compiler available for our evaluation during the course of this study. It seemed to have a level of sophistication similar to the VAX VMS or the IBM Hopt3. It is a very new compiler and detailed examination of some code shows both strengths (Sort) and weaknesses (FFT and Norm).

The compilers range from simple to the most sophisticated; differences that are discussed in the next chapter. A common compiler producing code for approximations to our architectures is discussed in Chapter 5.

3.2:   The Instruction Stream

In this section the instructions used to represent a program are examined and comparisons are made which include the CI measures. The first subsection examines the static size of the different machine representations for the test work load. The efficiency of a machine's representation is very important when determining cache and main memory requirements. The other subsection analyzes the dynamic instruction stream. The instruction stream produced by different architectures for an identical work load is quantitatively presented. The resource demands made by each machine are examined and compared with the CI representation.

3.2.1:   Static Size

The CI representation specifies the number of operations, operands, and labels necessary for a program. These items are encoded into syllables. Table 3.8 summarizes the static CI measures for the FFT

The following table summarizes the many representations of the test programs used in Chapters 3 and 4.

Architecture	Compiler Language	Remarks
VAX	UNIX portable F77	Simple. No register allocation. A little peephole optimization.
	VMS Fortran	Sophisticated and mature with many of the known optimization techniques.
PDP-11	UNIX portable C	Simple. No register allocation. A little peephole optimization.
P-Code	P-Code Pascal	Simple.
IBM S/370	Fortran G	Simple, with some peephole optimizations.
	Fortran Hopt0	Simple, with many redundant load and store instructions.
	Fortran Hopt1	Simple, with effective load/store elimination and loop control variables allocated to registers.
	Fortran Hopt2	Sophisticated and mature with most of the then-known optimization techniques (early 1960s).
	Fortran Hopt3	Sophisticated and mature with some algorithm changes that are little exposed by our test programs.
	Pascal/VS	At the time we measured this, it was a new product with only simple optimizations.
HP-PA	Fortran 77	Sophisticated but very early in its life cycle. Excellent local optimizations but not mature with full procedural optimization.

These compilers span a very wide range of capability. The reader should recognize that each has strong and weak points and should avoid the temptation to rank order the entire list. There are many examples of each compiler doing well in certain code sequences and poorly in others. Any effort to compare architectures must fully account for the influence of the compiler.

Table 3.8: Static CI measures for the FFT program.

Environment	CI Measures		
	Operations	Operands	Labels
MAIN	17	52	6
EXPTAB	37	59	3
RANDOM	6	8	0
FFT	35	63	5
Totals	95	182	14

program. For example, 17 operation syllables are necessary to represent the MAIN environment for the FFT program. The domain of an environment is left open in the derivation of the CI form. To determine the size of, say, the 17 syllables in MAIN, the size of each syllable is determined by using a uniform encoding of all unique operations in the environment. In this study, two different domains for the environments are presented. The first restricts the environment to a single procedure, and for the second, the environment spans the entire program. For the example, MAIN specifies nine unique operations, 17 unique operands, and five labels. Therefore, the size in bits necessary to represent the MAIN environment is:

$$\lceil \log_2 9 \rceil \times 17 + \lceil \log_2 17 \rceil \times 52 + \lceil \log_2 5 \rceil \times 6 = 352 \text{ bits (44 bytes)}$$

The total size when the environment is a subroutine is 1241 bits (156 bytes). If the environment is redefined to include the entire program and thereby fix the container sizes, the total size is 1613 bits (202 bytes). The 30 percent increase in the size of the program is not uniformly distributed among the three types of objects. Continuing with the FFT example, the operand containers represent 68 percent of the bits in the program. If the operand's environment is restricted to the subroutine and the operation and label environment is the program, then the static size increases by only 9.6 percent. Table 3.9 summarizes the static size measurements.

The size of a particular representation excludes the many run-time procedures and environmental supports that are not included in the CI measures. Table 3.10a shows very similar sizes for the S/370, VAX, and PDP-11 architectures. The P-code machine is noticeably worse than any other of the machines. The encoding mechanism used by the P-code architecture mapped each instruction to a single (four byte) word. If the encoding is changed to use one byte for instructions with no operands (e.g., add), and four bytes for all other instructions, the average savings is 18.3 percent. With that encoding the average relative program size is 8.2 times the CI value.

Table 3.9: CI static size.

	FFT	Mort	Norm	Sort	Avg.
CI static size; environment is a subroutine.	156 bytes	2451 bytes	2433 bytes	111 bytes	–
CI static size; environment is the program.	202 bytes	2628 bytes	3134 bytes	150 bytes	–
Percent increase.	30%	7.2%	29%	35%	25%
Percent increase when operand environment is a subroutine, operation and label environment is the program.	10%	2.4%	15%	17%	11%

The addressability of an architecture affects the static code size: the PDP-11 uses the smallest addresses, 16 bits, and is the most compact representation. Clearly the use of larger immediate addresses implies larger static program sizes. These effects appear to be small, since the values for S/370 Hopt1, VAX UNIX, and PDP-11 differ by only 16 percent, while the dynamic measures differ by a much larger amount.

The FFT values appear to be proportionally worse. The operations performed on complex data type operands are counted as a single CI operation, but no machine in the study has instructions that can reference complex data type objects.

For traditional architectures, a program's static size is relatively constant. Some studies [32,67] that have used the CI theory to synthesize new designs have dramatically reduced the static size by factors of two to four. Other efforts to reduce the size of a program's representation [3,64,66] have started with a given simple representation and then have been statistically optimized to form an enhanced representation that is more compact and executes fewer instructions. In a study of an architecture that supports a simple instruction set [50] the static program size was reported for several other architectures. Table 3.11 shows the averages for five simple procedures and five programs. The sum of all sizes is nearly 26K bytes; this is similar to the size of the test programs used in this book. Again, the program size is largely the same. All of these machines used the UNIX-based portable (simple) compiler. Our analysis shows that more sophisticated compilers can reduce this size.

Table 3.10: Static sizes.

(a) CI relative program size—simple compiler.

		FFT	Mort	Norm	Sort	Avg.
CI		1.00	1.00	1.00	1.00	1.00
S/370	Fortran Hopt1	8.63	3.82	5.57	6.90	6.23
P-Code	Pascal	13.62	6.13	10.66	10.09	10.12
VAX* UNIX	Fortran	9.99	3.62	4.75	7.24	6.40
PDP-11	C	9.04	2.78	4.69	5.19	5.43

*The values used for the VAX numbers were adjusted to account for the unnecessary use of long word displacement made for global variables when word displacement mode could have been used.

(b) CI relative program size—optimized compiler.

	FFT	Mort	Norm	Sort	Avg.
S/370	7.4	3.7	4.7	6.3	5.5
VAX/VMS	3.86	2.16	2.84	2.81	2.92
HP Precision	6.85	4.19	6.05	4.11	5.30

(c) Change in program size with simple and optimized compilation.

	Simple	Optimized	% Change
S/370	6.23	5.50	−12%
VAX	6.40	2.92	−54%

(d) Effect of CI weighting on relative program sizes.

	Average Weighted by CI Static Size	% Change
S/370	4.33	−21%
VAX/VMS	2.59	−11%
HP Precision	5.15	−3%

Table 3.11: Static size relative to RISC I architecture.

Machine	Size (Relative to RISC I)
RISC I	1.0
68000	.9
Z8002	1.2
VAX 11/780	.8
PDP 11/70	.9
BBN C/70	.7

Compiler Optimization

  The effect of optimization on relative program size can be seen in Figure 3.10b. Notice in particular the dramatic effect of optimization on the VAX architecture. Indeed, if we examine the percentage change due to optimization (Figure 3.10c), static size is decreased by 54% for VAX and by 12% for S/370. The relative effect of compilation on program size is not well understood, and subject to speculation in the literature. Much interest in advanced compiler optimization has focused on simple RISC-type instruction sets, with an apparent conclusion that compiler optimization can achieve the same effect as more complex instruction sets. What is occasionally lost is the fact that the more robust or complex instruction set also responds very well to compiler optimization. With relatively simple compiler techniques, VAX apparently is at par with the RISC-based HP-PA (Table 3.11), but with an optimized compiler the VAX code is less than half (.46) of the HP-PA code. Examination of code sequences from the HP-PA compiler shows many opportunities to reduce code size. It is not possible to estimate if improvements to the VAX code size would be also possible.

In another study [66], empirical high-level-language statistics were used to frequency encode operations. That effort reduced the static size by two to three times over conventional architectures typified by the PDP-11.

In efforts to reduce static program size, variable length instructions are often used. The VAX architecture is representative of that type of effort. The expected improvement in program size (non-optimized) is not shown by the statistics for a variety of reasons. The most critical was the inability of the software compilers and assemblers to generate the shortest form of an instruction. For example, the target of a call instruction is encoded as a program counter relative jump. The displacement can be a byte, word (16-bits), or long word (32-bits), but because of the many problems with separately compiled procedures the long word form is always used and rarely needed. The UNIX assembler properly generates short conditional and unconditional branches but does not attempt to use short displacements in procedure call instructions. A worse situation arises as the result of global variables. For language systems that allow for separately compiled modules, the global variable size cannot be determined until all modules are link-edited together. This is normally done after assembly and thus does not allow for the use of short address forms. While mechanisms to minimize the static size may exist, some of their features may make great demands on the system software. Fortunately, encoded branch displacements that allow long and short forms can be adequately utilized. Studies addressing the problem of variable-length instructions [54,65] conclude the problem is difficult, but when using certain constraints many parts of the problem can be solved in a reasonable time. The VAX values were adjusted to a more realistic value by assuming word displacement global references. The unadjusted values would increase the average relative program size to 7.0 (a 9 percent increase).

For most of the data used in this book, the four benchmark programs are averaged. However, several of the programs have small size and weighting each by its CI static size rather than simply averaging the four benchmarks may be more representative. For optimized compilers (Figure 3.10d), this reduces relative size between 3 and 21 percent. This gives some idea of the relative program size achievable in a mixed program environment.

Relative to the CI, the static size of a program's representation is very similar for several conventional architectures. The CI results indicate significant reductions are possible by using more efficient encoding techniques. The hardware tradeoffs between simple, inefficient instruction formats and complex, highly encoded instructions are constantly changing with technology.

3.2.2: Dynamic Analysis

The most basic measure of dynamic performance of an architecture is the number of instructions executed. Consider Table 3.12, which tabulates the total number of instructions executed for three different architectures (simple compilation). The instructions that executed in the user state were counted and scaled by the CI measure, operations, to form a relative count. To illustrate, for the FFT program the P-code machine executed 9.5 instructions for every CI operation executed in FFT. And overall the P-code machine executes 6.2 times the CI measures. These counts roughly correspond to job execution time. Often the total user state includes I/O buffering, memory allocation, system library execution, and other tasks performed in behalf of the program being monitored. For architectural comparisons, instructions that support very different run-time environments must be excluded.

The bounded monitor, described in Chapter 2, provides the precision that narrows the collected instruction stream. Table 3.13 and all subsequent tables show the results obtained by using bounded monitors. The number of excluded instructions can be quite large. In the case of the S/370 Pascal/VS compiler, the run-time environment managed a linked list of local frames allocated and deallocated on each procedure call and return. The architecture cannot be fairly compared to

Table 3.12: Instructions executed: total user state (per CI operation, simple compilation).

		FFT	Mort	Norm	Sort	Average
CI		1.0	1.0	1.0	1.0	1.0
S/370	Fortran Hopt1	5.0	2.7	4.5	2.1	3.6
P-Code	Pascal	9.5	4.3	7.3	3.8	6.2
VAX	Fortran	4.9	4.2	4.2	1.4	3.7

Table 3.13: Instructions executed: bounded monitors.

(a) Actual number of instructions executed (simple).

	FFT	Mort	Norm	Sort
CI	51256	2723073	634887	655042
S/370 Hopt1	221955	6017991	2406221	2143895
P-Code	428949	10278021	3714823	2521066
VAX	182632	3616960	1061428	925113
PDP-11	3211146	4887860	2314331	1367272

(b) Actual number of instructions executed (optimized).

	FFT	Mort	Norm	Sort
S/370 Hopt3	117889	4955992	799958	1133223
VAX/VMS	71820	–	515909	708404
HP Precision	141708	4311220	1566354	804240

others when this seemingly poor choice of a run-time environment is used. This linked-list approach is necessary for software compatibility to much older S/370 operating systems. Data from the Pascal/VS compiler will be presented in the next chapter.

Tables 3.13a and b present the actual number of instructions executed for each of the test programs with both simple and optimized compilation. Recall that the data from VAX/VMS were obtained from a monitor that was similar to the one used for UNIX, but with the important exception that it could not selectively ignore sections of the program so that I/O overhead could not be filtered out for some programs; thus, the data for Mort VAX/VMS are not available. The remainder of the programs do not use input and generate very limited output. The VAX VMS run-time environment has very little overhead for these programs and closely approximates what a bounded monitor would measure.

With simple compilation (Table 3.14a), there is approximately between two and five times the number of executed instructions per CI instruction. This drops noticeably with optimization to the range 1.1

Table 3.14: Instructions executed: bounded monitors (per CI operation).

(a) CI relative instruction count—simple compilation.

		FFT	Mort	Norm	Sort	Avg.
CI		1.0	1.0	1.0	1.0	1.0
S/370	Fortran Hopt1	4.27	2.21	3.79	2.11	3.10
P-Code	Pascal	8.37	3.78	5.85	3.85	5.46
VAX	UNIX Fortran	3.56	1.33	1.67	1.41	1.99
PDP-11	C	6.27	1.79	3.65	2.09	3.45

(b) CI relative instruction count—optimized compilation.

	FFT	Mort	Norm	Sort	Avg
S/370 Hopt3	2.30	1.82	1.26	1.73	1.78
VAX/VMS	1.40	–	.94	1.08	1.14
HP Precision	2.77	1.44	2.47	1.23	1.98

(c) Relative instruction count: optimized vs. naive.

	Naive	Optimized	% Change
S/370	3.1	1.78	−43%
VAX	1.99	1.14	−43%

(d) Relative instruction count weighted by CI instruction count (optimized only).

	Relative Count	% Change
S/370	1.72	−3%
VAX*	1.02	−11%
HP Precision	1.58	−20%

* Excluding MORT.

to 2. The percentage reduction due to optimization for those instruction sets where we have corresponding data (Table 3.14c) is exactly 43 percent for both S/370 and VAX. If we weight the programs in Table 3.14d by their CI instruction count rather than simply taking an average over the four test programs, there is about the same variance as with our static data (Table 3.10): from −11 percent to −20 percent.

Optimization on the HP Precision Architecture optimizer is very effective with certain programs, especially Sort. In examining the apparently poor instruction count of the Norm and FFT programs, a significant compiler difference was found. In the most executed doubly nested loop of the Norm program, the S/370 optimizer reduced the number of executed instructions by 50 percent (from about 16 to 11). This loop alone accounts for about 13 percent of the HP-PA executed instructions. It is not possible to estimate the total effect on the instruction stream. The HP-PA results also show a high use of integer multiplies. For this critical loop, the S/370 optimizer used "strength reduction" to eliminate the multiply.

Close examination of the FFT program found a similar difference. The HP-PA compiler does not use strength reduction to the extent that S/370 does and, in the critical inner loop, used several instructions to generate addresses. It also appears that the aliasing information and complex number code generation is not up to the maturity of the S/370 compilers. The next chapter further explores the effect of optimization on the instruction stream.

3.2.3:   Operation Specifiers and Formats

The executed instructions are grouped into categories first defined by Gibson [26]. Table 3.15 shows the results for the composite mix for the four machines. A composite mix scales the results for each program by the CI measures of operations and averages their sum. Tables that are not labeled as a specific program are always a composite mix. Because of the range of values, Table 3.15 is given relative to 1,000 CI operations. To illustrate, the S/370 Fortran H level 1 optimizer executes 1,489 Move instructions for every 1,000 CI operations.

The Gibson classes highlight many architectural features of the different machines. The P-code stack machine has a very large number of *move* (push, pop) instructions. The memory-to-memory VAX architecture performs the least number of *move* instructions. This is indicative of the larger number of addressing modes allowed by the VAX. The PDP-11 *move* figure is large, but when expressed as a percentage of total instructions the PDP-11 architecture ranks second smallest, just

Table 3.15: Gibson classification (per thousand CI operations).

Simple Compile

Gibson Class	S/370 Fortran Hopt1	P-Code Pascal	VAX Fortran	PDP-11 C
Move	1,489	3,664	391	1,259
Fix Add/Sub	276	1,016	694	755
Branch	263	252	227+59*	276
Shift	524	–	121	590
Compare	198	225	167	225
Floating-Point	246	254	234	251
Fix Multiply	76	12	80.5	73
Fix Divide	9.7	9.8	9.7	6.3
Conversion	–	14.5	10.3	9.9
Logical	10.6	6.7	–	–
Misc	–	3.0	–	10.5

Optimized Compile

Gibson Class	S/370 Fortran Hopt3	VAX/VMS	HP-PA
Move	858	262	871
Fix Add/Sub	140	161	394
Branch	264	197	257
Shift	123	–	83
Compare	128	112	10
Floating-Point	234	323	255
Fix Multiply	7.8	22	83
Fix Divide	10	5	–
Conversion	–	13	8
Logical	6	13	4
Misc	–	24	12

*Belongs to both *Fix Add/Sub* and *Branch* classes.

Instruction Measurements

Dynamic instruction count is a primary measure of an architecture's ability to efficiently execute programs. It is not the only measure, as we shall see later. Compilers have a significant effect on instruction count. Indeed, they have approximately the same effect as the architecture itself. Moving from a very simple instruction set to a very sophisticated one (consider P-code and VAX), we find about the same difference as in moving from a simple level of compilation to a sophisticated optimizing compiler.

As we have seen, static program size is a more secondary effect of architecture and optimization. As both architects and compiler writers strive to produce efficient program representations, they produce improved static program representation as a consequence. Static program size is not a trivial measure of efficiency. Ultimately, the cost of program execution is the space–time product of the program's lifetime in memory; some concern is warranted in creating a good static representation. On the other hand, more exotic techniques (Huffman encoded instructions, etc.) are almost never justified since their consequence on interpretation time is too great.

behind the VAX. Table 3.16 displays the Gibson classification percentages for Table 3.15.

It is important to remember that the PDP-11 floating-point architecture does not allow memory-to-memory operations but only supports memory-to-register instructions. For the relative value of 1,259 move instructions, 322 involved floating operand load and stores. The "Gibson" percentages for our test set seem typical of other studies [26,41]. The *branch* class frequency is lower than expected. This difference reflects the scientific work load used in this study. In a study of S/370 execution with scientific Fortran programs [59] branch frequencies ranged from 9.1 percent to 14.9 percent. Similar data can be collected for the optimized compiler environment (Tables 3.15b and 3.16b). Branching and floating-point operations form a noticeably higher percentage of optimized code than of non-optimized code. As we can see from Figures 3.15a and b, the amount of floating-point activity remains relatively constant not only across compilation, but also across architectures independent of compilation level.

As for the instructions that make up this Gibson Mix, a typical dynamically executed S/370 instruction generated by the Fortran Hopt1 compiler is a memory-to-register (RX format) instruction. The average length is 3.35 bytes and 67 percent of the instructions are four bytes long. The remainder are register-to-register (RR format) two-byte in-

Table 3.16: Gibson classification percentages.

Simple Compile

Gibson Class	S/370 Fortran Hopt1	P-Code Pascal	VAX Fortran	PDP-11 C
Move	48.1	67.1	19.6	36.5
Fix Add/Sub	8.9	18.6	34.8	21.9
Branch	8.5	4.6	14.4*	8.0
Shift	16.9	–	6.1	17.1
Compare	6.4	4.1	8.4	6.6
Floating-Point	7.9	4.7	11.7	7.3
Fix Multiply	2.5	.2	4.0	2.1
Fix Divide	.3	.2	.5	.2
Conversion	–	.3	.5	.3
Logical	.3	.1	–	–
Misc	–	.1	–	.3

Optimized Compile

Gibson Class	S/370 Fortran Hopt3	VAX/VMS	HP-PA
Move	48	23	44
Fix Add/Sub	7.8	14.1	19.9
Branch	15	17.3	13.0
Shift	6.9	0	4.2
Compare	7.2	9.8	.5
Floating-Point	13.5	28.3	12.9
Fix Multiply	.4	1.9	4.2
Fix Divide	.5	.4	0
Conversion	–	1.1	.4
Logical	.3	1.1	.2
Misc	–	2.1	.6

*Includes both *Fix Add/Sub* and *Branch* classes.

structions. All P-code instructions are four bytes long and the most common operation is loading from memory (31 percent). If the instruction set is recoded, as was done earlier in calculating a more realistic static size, then the average P-code instruction length is 3.49 bytes.

The VAX architecture allows the greatest flexibility in instruction formats. The instruction always begins with an opcode byte followed by operand specifiers. Operand specifiers always begin with a single-byte mode/register pair (or possible short immediate, termed literal), and are followed by additional values when needed. VAX instructions with no operands are one byte long. A complex three-operand instruction could be 16 or more bytes long. The typical instruction is an *add* (28 percent), while the next most frequent is a *move* (12 percent). Three-operand instructions eliminate the need to first load a value and then to operate on it. The average instruction length is 6.4 bytes (simple compilation). When this value is adjusted to use 2-byte displacements for global references (as explained earlier), the average size becomes 5.23 bytes. The PDP-11 instruction encoding is similar to the VAX except the mode qualifiers (immediate data, displacements) are grouped after all the mode/register pairs. PDP-11 instructions also are multiples of 2-byte words. The average PDP-11 instruction is 3.6 bytes long. Again the *move* instruction is most often encountered (27 percent). Tables 3.17a and b display the data for each of the machines relative to the CI measures.

While instructions and instruction bytes fetched per CI object decrease as optimization increases (S/370, Tables 3.17a and b), their ratio—the number of bytes per instruction—remains relatively constant: 3.35 for simple to 3.54 for optimized compilation. We can see the effect of optimization on instruction bandwidth in Table 3.17c. The I-bandwidth (relative to CI count) is useful to assess relative instruction traffic among various architectures. S/370 with optimized compilation (Table 3.17c) requires about 80 percent of the instruction bandwidth of the HP Precision Architecture (6.3 *vs.* 7.9 bytes/CI).

When interpreting an instruction, a machine fetches and decodes a portion of an instruction. In some cases the entire instruction can be captured; in other cases the interpretation of succeeding instruction parts is delayed until earlier parts are interpreted. Instruction objects are the non-overlapping portions of an instruction, which must be interpreted (decoded) before further instruction fragments can be interpreted. For example, the first 16 bits of an S/370 instruction is either an entire instruction or defines precisely the rest of that instruction. This definition does not require that each field (subgroup of bits) of an object be known, but does require that no part of one object be part of another object. This latter restriction applies to the VAX

Table 3.17: Instruction activities (per CI operation).

(a) Instruction activities (per CI operation)—simple compilation.

	S/370 Fortran Hopt1	P-Code Pascal	VAX Fortran	PDP-11 C
Instructions Fetched	3.10	5.46	1.99	3.45
Instruction Bytes Fetched	10.4	19.1*	10.4*	12.5
Instruction Objects Fetched	5.2	10.0*	9.2	6.0#

*Adjusted

Statistical estimate based on uniform distribution of *src/dst* mode specifiers.

(b) Instruction activities (per CI operation)—optimized compilation.

	S/370	VMS	HP
Instructions Fetched	1.78	1.14	1.98
Instruction Bytes Fetched	6.3	–	7.92
Instruction Objects Fetched	3.2	–	1.98

(c) Dynamic instruction bandwidth—optimized (average) I-bandwidth relative to instruction count.

	Bytes/I	Avg. CI Instr Count	I-Bandwidth Relative to CI Count
S/370 Hopt3	3.54	1.78	6.30
HP Precision	4.0	1.98	7.92

*See Table 4.19.

AUGUSTANA UNIVERSITY COLLEGE
LIBRARY

> **Instruction Bandwidth**
>
> Instruction bandwidth measures the number of bytes required for instructions to execute the program. It has two constituents: the average instruction size and the dynamic instruction count for program execution. As we shall see in Chapter 5, bandwidth directly determines the instruction cache size required to sustain a particular performance (miss rate). Smaller instruction bandwidth requirements mean smaller instruction caches.

architecture when it is known that the next, say, two bytes are part of the current instruction, but the second byte may be part of a long word displacement or perhaps the next mode/register specifier.

Instruction objects measure the number of interpretation cycles necessary to execute a program. It is possible for an implementation of an architecture to perform these interpretations in parallel by adding more hardware. For example, the S/370 architecture could always assume both an RX (32-bit) format instruction and an RR (16-bit) format instruction, by interpreting both possibilities. The incorrect interpretation could be aborted when the correct format was discovered. The VAX machine always decodes the second byte of an instruction as an operand specifier. Only for single-byte instructions and branch instructions is it necessary to abort the operand interpretation. If this added hardware is used, then the number of instruction objects would decline 21 percent to 7.2 objects per CI operation. Figure 3.1 shows the instruction objects executed for the composite mix by the VAX. GR corresponds to registers 0–11. FP, AP, SP, and PC refer to the frame pointer, argument pointer, stack pointer, and program counter registers, respectively. This table uses the operand notation used in the VAX architecture handbook [1].

Even though the VAX architecture executed the fewest instructions, it was necessary to interpret many more objects (Table 3.17a). Potential penalties for these excess objects depend on the implementation of the machine. There are alternatives to the VAX encoding that could reduce the problem. One simple mechanism would reorder the instruction so that all the register/mode specifiers are grouped after the opcode. Then the possible displacements, immediate values would be grouped at the end. In that way it would be possible to interpret all instructions, at worst, as three objects. All register-to-register or literal-to-register (5-bit immediate) instructions could be interpreted as two objects. As a worst-case estimate (simple compiler), the number of instruction objects for the composite mix would be 1.99×3 objects per CI operation. The actual test set value cannot be calculated since

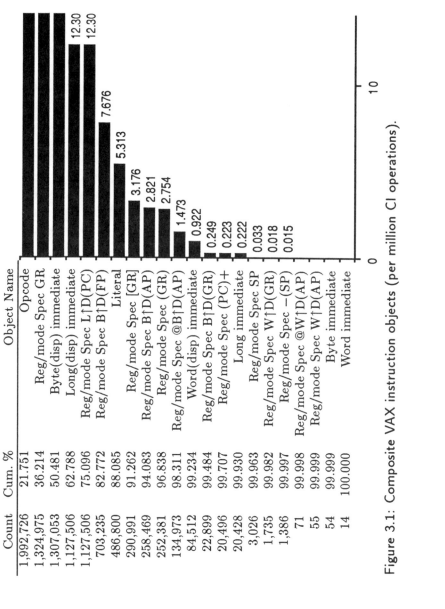

Count	Cum. %	Object Name	Value
1,992,726	21.751	Opcode	
1,324,975	36.214	Reg/mode Spec GR	
1,307,053	50.481	Byte(disp) immediate	
1,127,506	62.788	Long(disp) immediate	12.30
1,127,506	75.096	Reg/mode Spec L↑D(PC)	12.30
703,235	82.772	Reg/mode Spec B↑D(FP)	7.676
486,800	88.085	Literal	5.313
290,991	91.262	Reg/mode Spec [GR]	3.176
258,469	94.083	Reg/mode Spec B↑D(AP)	2.821
252,381	96.838	Reg/mode Spec (GR)	2.754
134,973	98.311	Reg/mode Spec @B↑D(AP)	1.473
84,512	99.234	Word(disp) immediate	0.922
22,899	99.484	Reg/mode Spec B↑D(GR)	0.249
20,496	99.707	Reg/mode Spec (PC)+	0.223
20,428	99.930	Long immediate	0.222
3,026	99.963	Reg/mode Spec SP	0.033
1,735	99.982	Reg/mode Spec W↑D(GR)	0.018
1,386	99.997	Reg/mode Spec −(SP)	0.015
71	99.998	Reg/mode Spec @W↑D(AP)	
55	99.999	Reg/mode Spec W↑D(AP)	
54	99.999	Byte immediate	
14	100.000	Word immediate	

Figure 3.1: Composite VAX instruction objects (per million CI operations).

Instructions Executed vs. Objects Executed

Table 3.17 highlights the advantage and disadvantage of an architecture such as VAX. With both register and memory-to-memory formats, it is possible to achieve significant reductions in the number of instructions required to execute a program compared to load–store machines or even to register-memory-only machines. The availability of an extended set of formats reduces the dynamic instruction count, bringing it close to the CI measure.

In the case of VAX, however, this advantage came with a high price tag—a significant increase in the number of "instruction objects" fetched and executed. One can view the "instruction objects" category in Table 3.17 as akin to the number of decodes required to execute a program. Additional decoding effort is required when instructions have variable size; each instruction must be decoded to determine the starting point of the subsequent instruction. When this is simply done (in the primary instruction categories for System 370, there are only two sizes of major interest) the machine can, with extra hardware, decode both potential sizes simultaneously. In the case of VAX, there is the possibility of up to 19 different instruction sizes and determination of an instruction size may require five sequential decode steps. Thus, the number of objects fetched for the VAX is twice that of System 370, while it executes two-thirds the number of instructions (Table 3.17a). Reducing the number of instructions executed by increasing the number of instruction formats available does not necessarily require a significant increase in the number of instruction objects executed. This latter category is a result of variability of instruction size and the use of "mode decodes" to determine that size.

operand pair and triple data were not collected. HP-PA has the simplest encoding of instruction objects: all 32 bits. This results in the least number of instruction objects for the machine to interpret. This is one of the advantages of RISC style architectures, and is an important consideration in machine design.

3.2.4: *Register and Address Specification*

Register sets and stacks are the two traditional mechanisms to hold intermediate and often used values. The number of registers is usually small to allow short specifiers in the instructions and high speed access. Stack architectures eliminate source and destination specifiers when referencing the stack, and allow very short instructions. Tables 3.18a and b show the number of register and stack references for each architecture relative to the number of instructions executed.

Table 3.18: Register references (per executed instruction).

(a) Simple

		FFT	Mort	Norm	Sort	Avg.
S/370	Fortran Hopt1	2.43	2.04	2.41	2.15	2.26
P-Code	Pascal	2.26	2.13	2.22	2.16	2.20
VAX/UNIX	Fortran	2.51	1.90	2.83	2.03	2.32
PDP-11	C	2.31	1.74	2.31	1.86	2.06

(b) Optimized

S/370	Fortran Hopt3	—	—	—	—	2.49
VAX/VMS	Fortran	4.16	—	3.81	1.90	3.29
HP Precision	Fortran	2.70	2.12	2.51	2.64	2.49

Table 3.19: Register and immediate references (per CI operation).

(a) Simple compilation.

		References	
		Register	Immediate
S/370	Fortran Hopt1	7.1	–
P-Code	Pascal	12.1	–
VAX/UNIX	Fortran	4.8	.5
PDP-11	C	7.5	.6

(b) Optimized compilation.

		Average
S/370	Fortran Hopt3	4.43
VAX/VMS		3.75
HP-PA		4.93

Register accesses for effective address calculations and references to the program counter were included except for immediate values and normal instruction sequencing. In this way the VAX and PDP-11 immediate mode does not count as a reference, but a program counter (PC) relative address counts as a read reference to the program counter. The conditional branch target is one example of PC relative addressing. For the PDP-11 and VAX, implicit use of the stack pointer register counts as a register read and write since it is not a true stack and must allow arbitrary modification of the stack pointer register. Notice that as optimization increases (Tables 3.18a and b), the register references per executed instruction increase, indicating better usage of the register set.

The use of the stack pointer itself is not counted for the P-code machine. For example, an integer add instruction counts as two read references and one write reference. The P-code machine has no registers except a *display* used to address variables, the program counter, and a storage pointer.

The data indicate a remarkable similarity (simple compilation) between each of the architectures. The average values differ by, at worst, 11 percent. The specific distribution of register references for each instruction was not collected. The simplest and shortest instruction (by reference) is a branch. The S/370 architecture allows two references to a base register and to a index register that is rarely used. The PDP-11, VAX, and P-code architectures all use PC relative branches, which again results in a single read reference. In nearly all cases the operands for an instruction either exist in a register or use a register that participates in an effective address calculation. The introduction of immediate operands in the VAX and PDP-11 machines does not significantly reduce the register reference frequency. Immediate operands in a composite mix (scaled by the CI operation measure) are summarized in Table 3.19. The frequency of immediate operands is low enough that other factors overwhelm the savings in register references introduced by immediate values. These values do not argue for or against immediate operands but serve to quantify register traffic requirements for machine designers. Again, as optimization increases, the effect (Tables 3.19a and b) is to reduce the total number of register references but increase the references per instruction (Table 3.18).

Register references are either data for operands or addresses for address calculations. The breakdown of register read references for addresses is given in Table 3.20.

In all cases, shift operations were used to scale registers for use in array address calculations. These register references are counted as

Table 3.20: Register address references.

S/370	Fortran Hopt1	56%[1]
P-Code	Pascal	67%[2]
VAX/UNIX	Fortran	87%[1]
PDP-11	C	84%[1]

[1] Includes shift instruction.
[2] Includes DEC (decrease top of stack) instruction references.

an address reference. The P-code machine used the DEC (decrease top of stack) instruction to generate biased array pointers. For this reason, the stack references for the DEC instruction are counted as address references. There are many instances of address arithmetic that are not detected, the fraction of address references is therefore a conservative estimate and may be considerably higher. Although the S/370, PDP-11, and VAX architectures have designed the register set to be general purpose, the majority of the references to registers use the contents as addresses. Therefore, the effective address generation cycles of a machine make the highest use of register contents. Even excluding the shift instructions, the VAX architecture references 83 percent of all register read references during effective address computation.

The mechanism used to reference objects in main memory centers around the calculation of an effective address. In the S/370 architecture all memory addresses are generated by summing an optional base register, an optional index register, and a positive displacement. The distribution of base and index registers is shown in Table 3.21 for the composite mix by the S/370 Fortran Hopt1 compiler. The skew in the base and index register distributions is noticeable. The final 6 registers represent 91 percent of all base register references; the four most referenced registers include 86 percent of the references. A typical memory-to-register operation uses a register as one source and the destination. The single source/destination register specifier has a skewed distribution such that the four most heavily used registers account for 76 percent of all references.

The non-uniformity of register references is used in the design of the VAX and PDP-11 architectures. Since the software often assigns specific functions to registers these architectures predefined several registers. Rather than generate a self-relative pointer for branch target addressing, the program counter is used in address calculations. Advances in storage management, including virtual memories, allow very simple stack organizations for block structured languages. The designation of a register as a hardware stack pointer allows many optimizations. The

Table 3.21: S/370 address registers (per thousand CI operations).

	Register Use	
	Index	Base
Excluded	956	4.5
R1	–	3.9
R2	248	1.1
R3	322	2.7
R4	15.5	3.1
R5	7.0	0.2
R6	–	7.6
R7	–	11
R8	–	145
R9	–	106
R10	–	115
R11	–	251
R12	–	36
R13	–	824
R14	0.2	–
R15	–	38

P-code machine uses the stack for all expression evaluation. Since the locations of the operands are known it is not necessary to specify the stack pointer in the instruction. In an architecture carefully encoded to produce compact code, significant savings were realized by dedicating general registers to specific environment pointers [37,64].

The VAX architecture designates the stack, frame, and argument pointers and program counter as general registers. Many important instructions make implicit references to specific registers. The most common is PC relative addressing used in branch instructions. Interrupts implicitly use the stack and the general procedure call instruction updates all of these registers. Table 3.22 summarizes the register fetches encountered by the VAX architecture for the composite mix. If register references were uniform, then the expected frequency would be 1/16th, or about 6 percent. The registers R0–R11 would be expected to account for 75 percent of all references. The program counter is the most referenced register. Immediate values (including the "literal" mode) are not included. In addition to referencing instruction branch targets, the PC is used to reference global data. As indicated before, this has an unfortunate side effect of requiring long displacements (4 bytes) when shorter displacements would be possible. The use of a global pointer would have been more effective.

The few references to the stack pointer is surprising. In defining a frame pointer and argument pointer, the need for a stack pointer by

Register Class	Percent
General Register R0–R11	31.9
Frame Pointer	19.0
Stack Pointer	.4
Program counter	37.5

the user state is minimized. In many block structured languages it is possible to eliminate the stack pointer and still to allow expression evaluation on a pseudo stack. In the VAX architecture each dedicated register is automatically saved and restored during a procedure call. For languages that use the stack to pass arguments, it would be simple to eliminate the argument and stack pointers.

The PDP-11 stack pointer references are also infrequent. In only 0.3 percent of the instruction operand specifiers is the stack used. The stack pointer's traditional use in interrupt handlers is circumvented by the PDP-11 and VAX, since an alternate stack pointer is substituted for the user's stack pointer. It is evident from these data that a register machine does not need a stack evaluation mechanism. Local variable and procedure call requirements usually can be provided by a single environment pointer.

3.2.5: Displacements and Immediates

The operand specifiers found in the VAX and PDP-11 instruction stream are fundamentally the same as those of the S/370. In each case, to reference memory, a register is added to an immediate displacement field that points to the operand. When arrays are indexed, additional arithmetic is required. Table 3.23 summarizes the explicit operand specifiers found in the PDP-11 instruction stream.

Of the operand specifiers that reference objects in main memory, not including the instruction stream itself, 93 percent of all references are of the *base-displacement* type (base register plus a displacement field in the instruction). Table 3.24 summarizes the explicit operand specifiers found in the VAX instruction stream. For each reference to main memory, the base-displacement address mechanism accounts for 80 percent of the references.

The size of the displacement fields vary among the different architectures. The P-code machine allows 18 bits, the S/370 architecture 12, and the PDP-11 uses 16. The VAX architecture encodes its instructions based on the fact that few values are used. The shortest

Table 3.23: PDP-11 operand specifier distribution.

Operand Specifiers	FFT	Mort	Norm	Sort	Average
Register	37.5	39.7	34.8	43.6	38.9
Stack or Frame Pointer + Disp.	35.1	33.0	36.9	39.7	36.2
General Register + Displacement	7.3	15.5	2.0	11.4	9.1
Program Counter + Displacement	.3	7.0	1.8	1.1	2.6
Immediate Value or Address	14.1	4.4	15.5	4.2	9.6
Register as Address	5.5	.1	8.4	–	3.5
Register as Address with Auto Inc/Dec	.2	.2	.6		.3

Table 3.24: VAX operand specifier distribution.

Operand Specifiers	FFT	Mort	Norm	Sort	Average
Register	30.2	16.9	36.9	20.4	26.1
Frame or Argument Pointer + Disp.	35.9	.6	24.8	1.0	15.6
General Register + Displacement	.2	–	1.8	–	.5
Program Counter + Displacement	9.4	57.5	22.4	49.3	34.7
Immediate Value or Address	13.1	7.8	3.1	17.8	10.5
Register as Address	11.1	17.2	10.7	11.4	12.6
Register as Address with Auto Inc/Dec	–	–	.1	–	–

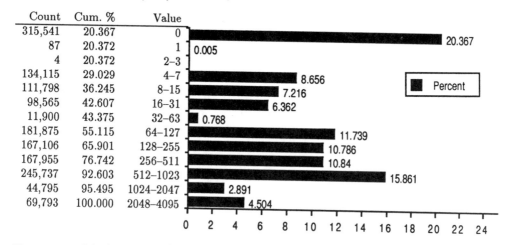

Count	Cum. %	Value
315,541	20.367	0
87	20.372	1
4	20.372	2–3
134,115	29.029	4–7
111,798	36.245	8–15
98,565	42.607	16–31
11,900	43.375	32–63
181,875	55.115	64–127
167,106	65.901	128–255
167,955	76.742	256–511
245,737	92.603	512–1023
44,795	95.495	1024–2047
69,793	100.000	2048–4095

Figure 3.2: Displacement field distribution (per million CI operations).

displacement field is 8 bits, and longer fields of 16 and 32 bits are allowed. In Table 3.24 less than 1 percent of the displacements require 16 bits. The long word (4-byte) displacements used by the PC relative operand specifiers reflect the software problem explained earlier. To gain insight into the displacement field size needed by global references, consider the S/370 displacement field histogram in Figure 3.2. This displays the number of bits utilized by the 12-bit displacement field for all of the register-to-memory (RX) instructions. These data indicate a field larger than one byte is necessary to capture the global references using base-displacement addressing. In another study of the VAX instruction stream [72] the frequency of word (2-byte) displacements was very small, but long word (4-byte) displacements accounted for 29 percent of all displacements for three Bliss language programs. It is not likely that optimization was used to shorten the global references. In any event, these data indicate the effectiveness of a single-byte displacement for arguments and local variables and indicate the need for longer displacements and/or more sophisticated hardware and software techniques for global referencing.

Often the operands for an instruction are not specified as registers, statements, or memory locations, but rather the value of the operand is encoded into the instruction. The simplest method is to imply the value of a constant in the opcode. A clear or increment instruction illustrates this. The S/370 architecture does not provide any mechanism of this type, except the branch on count (BCT) instruction. BCT subtracts one from a register and conditionally branches. For a clear instruction, it is necessary to zero a register by subtraction and to store the created zero in the appropriate memory location. There are several other methods to clear objects that depend on the size of memory to be cleared. In each case the machine designers attempted to optimize the speed of execution. For example, the move character (MVC) instruction is used to clear larger (< 256 bytes) areas of memory by overlapping source and destination to propagate a single zero byte through the entire block. As a result, the high-speed implementations of the S/370 architecture especially decode that type of MVC instruction and optimize its execution.

The PDP-11 and VAX machines include specific instructions to clear and increment or decrement a location. In 3.9 percent of the composite mix for PDP-11 and 1.2 percent of the VAX instructions, implied operands were used. For the VAX figure an additional 14.6 percent of the instructions used an implied shift value in the address calculation that shifts a quantity before adding to some base address. The shift amount is based on the type of operands (e.g., byte, word, or long word).

Replacing the operand specifier with the value itself requires little extra space in the instruction stream. Immediate operands are rarely used in the S/370 architecture but are quite common in the P-code, PDP-11, and VAX machines. S/370 immediate operands are restricted to length specifiers and optionally to certain address calculations. The load address (LA) instruction allows the programmer to perform address calculations and save the result. Unfortunately, only 24-bit arithmetic is performed and there is no overflow detection. The shift operators use the result of a base + displacement address calculation to specify the number of positions to shift. Figure 3.3 summarizes the shift values when the base register was specified as zero (i.e., excluded). The *31 or greater* entry results from the sign extension of registers for division. Only a few values account for all use of the shift count. The shift instructions could be encoded as RR type (16-bit) instructions where the shift size is placed in a 4-bit field (with a zero value indicating sign extension). All observed shift sizes would be included and an escape mechanism could signal for an additional word. This change would reduce the dynamic instruction size by 10 percent. This also indicates that full shift networks are unnecessary for this work load and compiler environment.

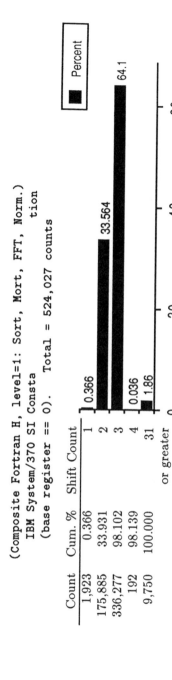

(Composite Fortran H, level=1: Sort, Mort, FFT, Norm.)
IBM System/370 SI Consta   tion
(base register == 0).   Total = 524,027 counts

Count	Cum. %	Shift Count	
1,923	0.366	1	0.366
175,885	33.931	2	33.564
336,277	98.102	3	64.1
192	98.139	4	0.036
9,750	100.000	31	1.86
		or greater	

■ Percent

Figure 3.3: S/370 shift count (per million CI operations).

The P-code architecture uses immediate operands in several instructions. The field normally used for displacements can be designated an 18-bit immediate value. The increase (INC), decrease (DEC), and load constant (LDC) instructions use the immediate field as expected. Two other instructions use the immediate field in address calculations. The indexed address (IXA) instruction scales the element on the top of the stack by the immediate value and adds this to the element below the top of the stack. These immediate values represent array element sizes used by the programs. A final instruction that uses the immediate field is the index and push instruction (IND). IND adds the immediate field to the address on the top of the stack and fetches that object. Figure 3.4 summarizes the immediate fields used by these instructions. Again, a very limited range of multipliers is used by the array indexing instruction (IXA). The constants zero and one appear in 41 percent of the immediate operands. The DEC instruction is used to create a biased index for arrays that do not begin at zero. Using a biased array base would eliminate all of the DEC instructions encountered by the P-code machine. Also the constant zero used by the IND instruction is used to perform a simple indirect access by using the element on the top of the stack. This reference could have been supported with a separate opcode if shorter instruction formats were used. If these unnecessary references to zero and one were excluded, then the constant values zero and one would only comprise 20 percent of the immediate values. These data indicate that the disproportionate frequency of certain constants is due to the run-time environment requirements. Improvements in the compiler and run-time environment would reduce the frequency of specific constant values and would diminish expected performance gains from frequency encoding constants. As a final measure of immediate fields, 22.5 percent of the source operands are constants generated from an immediate field, 51.0 percent are stack references, and 26.5 percent are main memory references. These values are very sensitive to the compiler and change greatly as sophisticated optimization is used.

The PDP-11 architecture uses a 16-bit immediate field. Immediate operands represent 7.5 percent of all instruction source operands. Main memory and registers account for 28.7 percent and 63.8 percent of the source operands, respectively. If memory and immediate source operand fetches are grouped together, then immediate operands account for 20.7 percent of the references. Thus, the architectural attribute of immediate values reduces memory read traffic for the PDP-11 by 20.7 percent. For the P-code machine, memory traffic is reduced 45.9 percent by the use of immediates.

The VAX architecture encodes immediate values in two ways. Values from 0 to 63 are stored as a single byte, and termed *literals*. Values

Constant Encoding

A great deal of attention has been paid to the encoding of constants into the instruction set for modern architectures. It has been recognized that constant values of zero and one are particularly important. Our data indicate that a disproportionate number of certain constants is due to the run-time environment, and that improvements in both the compiler and the run-time environment reduce the frequency of the use of constants significantly.

In creating an instruction set, it is important for the architect to recognize trends in compiler optimization and in operating systems so that the instruction set investment may be made in the area of maximum performance return. The appearance of sophisticated register allocators has significantly impacted instruction set design. Registers finally can be effectively used. As a consequence, stack architectures have faded from the scene.

Register allocators primarily reduce read traffic. Write traffic remains little affected, except in unusual cases where the initial allocation itself was quite poor.

outside of this range require a one-byte specifier and the value. The length of the immediate field is determined by the implied type of the operator. For the composite work load, 96 percent of immediate values were literals. In another study of the VAX architecture [72] compiler execution written in Bliss used literals for at least 82 percent of the immediate operands. That study grouped immediate references with some other references, so the actual percentage is somewhat higher. For the VAX, 7.7 percent of the source operand references were immediate values. Again, if immediate values and memory references are grouped together then 18.5 percent are immediate references.

Immediate values are an effective mechanism to reduce memory traffic. The number of different constants referenced in the source representation of the program is much smaller than the immediate traffic would suggest. Compiler organization and optimization has a much greater effect on the values and frequency of immediate operands. It is necessary to consider the compilers that will be used in order to design the structure of immediate operands within an architecture.

3.3: Memory Referencing

High-level-language compilers map program variables into the storage that is available on the target architectures. The most straightforward approach uses a homogeneous storage area large enough to hold all

(Composite P-code Pascal: Sort, Mort, FFT, Norm.)
Immediate specifiers (by instruction).
Total = 2,150,834 counts

Count	Cum. %	Instruction	Percent
667,077	31.014	INC -1	31.0
15,086	31.716	INC 1	0.701
2,156	31.816	INC 4:7	0.1
24,332	32.947	INC 8:15	1.131
371,758	50.232	IND 0	17.284
2,156	50.332	IND 4:7	0.1
83,567	54.217	IND 8:15	3.885
79	54.221	IXA 1	0.003
176,243	62.415	IXA 4:7	8.194
165,147	70.093	IXA 8:15	7.678
255,721	81.983	IXA 16:31	11.889
66,728	85.085	IXA 128:255	3.102
30,534	86.505	LDC 0	1.419
183,403	95.032	LDC 1	8.527
31,211	96.483	LDC 2:3	1.451
18,359	97.336	LDC 4:7	0.853
11,318	97.863	LDC 8:15	0.526
4,517	98.073	LDC 16:31	0.21
257	98.085	LDC 32:63	0.011
14,652	98.766	LDC 64:127	0.681
6,206	99.054	LDC 128:255	0.288
1,371	99.118	LDC 256:511	0.063
6,317	99.412	LDC 1024:2047	0.293
6,322	99.706	LDC 4096:8191	0.293
6,317	100.000	LDC 8K:16K	0.293

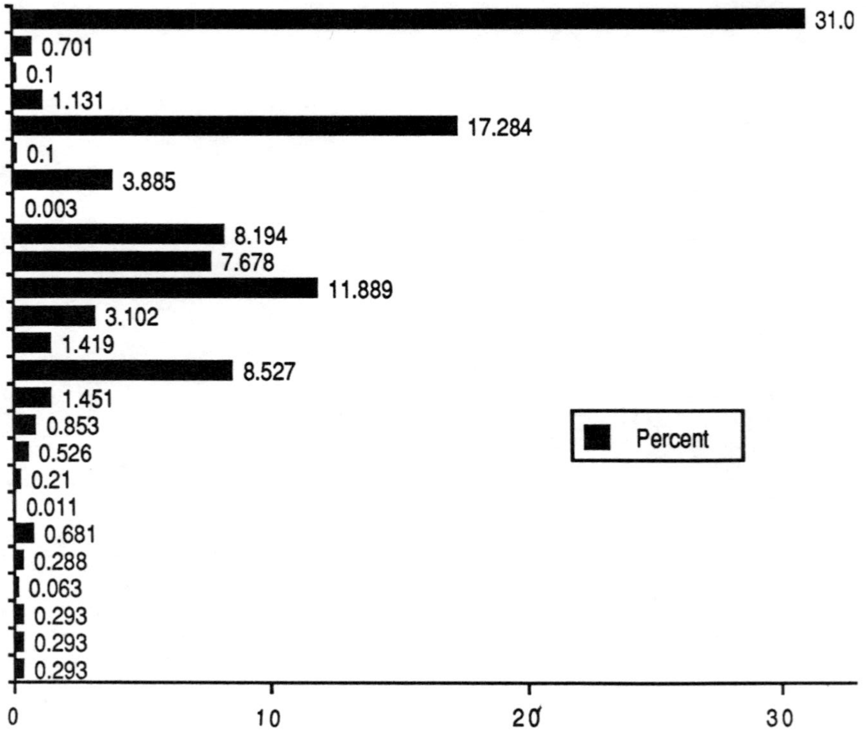

Figure 3.4: P-code immediate values (per million CI operations).

variables. This region is usually main memory, but some interpretive systems [53] have defined variable storage outside of the registers and main memory of the machine. Mapping program variables to high speed storage mechanisms (i.e., registers) requires more sophisticated compiler techniques. In this section memory referencing behavior for simpler compilers is examined. Most program variables are mapped to main memory, but intermediate results and various run-time objects may be in registers or evaluation stacks. The S/370 Hopt1 compiler allocates array names and loop indices to registers.

3.3.1: Address Generation

Computer architectures use many mechanisms to reference program variables. The CI measure for variables referenced indicates the number of program variables specified by the program. Table 3.25 summarizes the number of memory reads for the test set on the different architectures. In some cases the CI measure is bettered because the architecture can avoid memory reads for constants, array base addresses, and loop variables. Mechanisms, such as immediate values, are architectural features that reduce memory traffic and make a more efficient machine. Notice that data referencing is largely a property of register set size and register allocation policy rather than instruction set architecture. VAX and S/370 with 16 registers should be expected to produce the same memory read activity given the same register allocator. Clearly (Table 3.25b), there is a great deal of variability with a VAX optimizer producing less data traffic than S/370 for Sort, but considerably more for FFT and Norm programs. As expected, the HP Precision instruction set with 32 registers produces (with only one exception) the minimum memory data read traffic.

Table 3.26 summarizes the number of memory stores for the test set. The values for the write traffic are in close agreement with the CI measures (simple compilation). The VAX architecture appears slightly worse for three of the programs but is over three times the expected value for the FFT program. In examining the code produced, there are two main reasons for this anomaly. First, the code-to-index complex arrays used a compiler created variable (CCV) in main memory to hold an intermediate address calculation. Also, intermediate floating-point results appear to only use registers 0, 2, and 4, and then overflow into CCV's in the stack frame. For complex floating-point, three registers hold one complete value, and nearly all complex arithmetic overflows into the stack frame. When these references are excluded, the number of main memory stores is reduced to 32,347. Optimization on System 370 (Table 3.26b) shows little effect on data write traffic, but noticeable effect for certain programs on the VAX. The FFT and the Sort program—the smallest of the test programs—had data write traffic reduced by a factor of 5:1. Again as expected, the HP Precision Architecture with 32 registers produces (again with a few exceptions) the minimum data write traffic.

Earlier discussion of the dynamic characteristics of the programs indicate that, on the average, 26.1 percent of the program references were array references. S/370 main memory read and write traffic was, for the simple compiler, superior to all of the other architectures and the CI measures. As indicated before, the improvement is the result of the compiler that uses improved register allocation techniques. Nearly all (> 90 percent) memory references use the RX format register-to-memory instructions. The memory address is the summation of the contents of an index register, base register, and a 12-bit positive immediate field. Base and index registers can be excluded from the calculation by specifying "no register" (i.e., 0) in the appropriate field. As shown earlier in this chapter, the base register is included in nearly all references. Of these, 38.3 percent included an index register. The D-field distribution discussed earlier was non-zero 80 percent of the time. In examining the code produced by the Fortran Hopt1 compiler, some of the memory references that used an index register used a zero D-field. For array references of the form *array name [variable + constant]*, the addition of the constant was performed by placing the correct value into the D-field.

The index register is only used by this compiler for array references and reflects an important effect of register architectures. While the source program specified 26.1 percent array references, register allocation (in this case, quite simple methods) by the compiler significantly raised the frequency of array accesses to main memory. The work load in this study contains a higher frequency of array access than typical of systems programming, but the effect is present in all work loads. In another study of high-level-language program execution [50], 25 percent of the program references were to arrays and structures. The work load for that study ranged from compilers to VLSI design aids.

The P-code architecture uses two mechanisms to address objects in main memory. Simple variables are addressed by using a *display*. The display is an array of addresses that point to the most recent activation record for each level of static nesting. An address is specified as a pair: the static nesting level and a displacement into that activation record. Since the work load used in this study was derived from Fortran programs, only global and local references could occur. This mechanism is equivalent to the base-displacement mechanism used by S/370.

Table 3.25: Memory object reads.

(a) Simple

		FFT	Mort	Norm	Sort
CI		104,512	4,695,823	1,235,963	1,243,603
S/370	Fortran Hopt1	71,501	2,926,849	638,385	369,326
P-Code	Pascal	194,291	3,054,908	1,493,070	1,062,216
VAX UNIX	Fortran	202,853	2,975,244	1,458,185	824,856
PDP-11	C	206,660	3,043,367	1,452,330	771,243

(b) Optimized

S/370	51,000	2,208,000	397,000	292,000*
VAX/VMS	80,095	—	854,067	187,196
HP Precision	45,257	1,448,618	340,851	187,473

* To nearest thousand.

Table 3.26: Memory object writes.

(a) Simple

		FFT	Mort	Norm	Sort
CI		22,459	567,463	207,573	246,665
S/370	Fortran Hopt1	28,583	586,084	177,709	97,120
P-Code	Pascal	23,357	556,242	209,878	246,665
VAX UNIX	Fortran	71,031	666,794	271,272	248,873
PDP-11	C	30,162	586,474	258,145	247,056

(b) Optimized

S/370	Fortran Hopt3	24,000	614,000	156,000	108,000*
VAX/VMS	Fortran	14,813	—	258,294	80,200
HP Precision	Fortran	20,278	479,061	278,904	58,491

* To nearest thousand.

3.3. MEMORY REFERENCING

Table 3.27: P-code memory references (average per million CI operations).

Access Using	Number of Memory References
Display	1,902,061
Calculated Address	656,170

Table 3.28: Reference address generation (average percentage).

	PDP-11	VAX
Register as Address	7.4	7.0
Register Plus Displacement	89.0	73.9
Absolute	–	5.7
Indirect Plus Displacement	3.6	3.9
Index	–	9.4

Addresses can also be calculated. The same mechanism used for expressions can be employed to generate an address. Table 3.27 summarizes the relative number of memory references. Because the P-code machine cannot optimize commonly used variables, the fraction of calculated addresses (25.7 percent) quite closely matches the value indicated by the high-level-language representation (26.1 percent).

The PDP-11 and VAX architectures use quite similar mechanisms to access main memory. The instruction specifies operands by using a mode/register pair. Occasionally, the mode field that specifies the interpretation of the register field is implied by the operation field. The mode/register pair may specify operands as register contents, immediate fields, or may generate a main memory address used to fetch or store operands. Main memory addresses may be the contents of registers or displacements added to registers much like the S/370 architecture. The PDP-11 does not support the addition of two registers, which S/370 allows. The VAX architecture includes a mode, termed *index mode*, which adds potentially scaled register contents to another address. By using this *index mode*, the base + index + displacement operation of the S/370 can be performed by the VAX. In addition, the index register can be scaled by 1, 2, 4, or 8 to simplify array indexing. The PDP-11 and VAX allow indirect addressing. The memory element pointed to by the address calculation contains the address of the operand. A special case of indirect addressing is the *absolute* mode, specifying an immediate operand as an address. Table 3.28 summarizes the address specifiers used by the PDP-11 and VAX architectures for the average when reading operands.

As expected, the register plus displacement mode occurs most frequently. The PDP-11 only uses 16-bit displacement fields for operand references and the VAX allows 8, 16, and 32-bit fields. References to objects using the argument pointer and frame pointer account for 39.4 percent of all read memory references. All of these references that use the frame pointer (local variables) employ 8-bit offsets. All but .002 percent of the argument pointer (arguments) references used 8-bit displacement fields. In another study of the VAX architecture [72] the frequency of 16-bit displacement modes was 1.5 percent and total frequency of displacement modes was 22.8 percent (includes all operand specifiers for a mix of Bliss programs).

From these data, the mechanism most used to read main memory objects by all of the architectures in this study is "base + displacement." The VAX data indicate that a 8-bit displacement field is adequate for local and argument references, but references to global data may require larger offsets. The address generation mechanisms for memory write traffic is similar to that explained for the read traffic. This only major difference was a dramatic reduction in the use of the argument pointer. It seems that arguments are more often read than written. Many parameters could have been passed by value. An interprocedural global optimizer for Fortran would benefit from observing read-only operands and passing values instead of addresses.

3.3.2: Memory Operands

There are few data types allowed by the Fortran language. Table 3.29 summarizes the number of each data type for memory read operands. The *Other* category groups character, Boolean, and variable length memory objects. The P-code, PDP-11, and VAX numbers are quite close to the CI expected value of 1.89 memory references per CI operation. The number of real objects read was similar for all of the architectures. But the nearly two-thirds reduction in integer references by the S/370 architecture can only be attributed to the compiler. While it is true that the S/370 executed 50 percent more instructions than the VAX in the composite mix, it referenced only half as many memory objects. Perhaps as surprising, the PDP-11 executed 70 percent more instructions than the VAX, yet referenced nearly the same number of memory objects. The high-level-language programs require a certain amount of variable references. The machine architecture may map these variable references to any of several storage mechanisms (e.g., registers, main memory, cache). The S/370 has a similar mechanism to the VAX to allocate program variables and all of the improvement in reference behavior can be traced to the compiler. The real data refer-

Table 3.29: Memory reads by data type (per CI operation).

(a) Simple

		Integer	Address	Real	Other	Total
S/370	Fortran Hopt1	.57	–	.42	.02	1.01
P-Code	Pascal	1.36	.50	.36	–	2.22
VAX	Fortran	1.5	.14	.46	–	2.15
PDP-11	C	1.74	.04	.37	–	2.15

(b) Optimized

		Integer	Address	Real	Other	Total
S/370	Fortran Hopt4	.38		.32	.02	.72
VAX/VMS	Fortran	.71	–	.35	–	1.06
HP Precision	Fortran	.23	–	.33		.56

ences are usually to array elements. Since none of the machines offered a faster storage mechanism than main memory for large data objects (e.g., arrays), the references specified by the program must occur during the execution of the program. The *Address* column of Table 3.29a is a conservative estimate of the number of addresses fetched. The S/370, PDP-11, and VAX architectures use a mixture of integer and address operations when calculating and using addresses. On the other hand, the P-code machine directly maps source address loads. The .50 address references per CI operation represent 23 percent of the memory references and agree well with the 26 percent array accesses indicated by the high-level-language source. Compiler optimization (Table 3.29b) reduces the data memory traffic as expected. The Precision Architecture with 32 registers requires fewer memory reads than VAX or S/370. Notice that the reduction in traffic comes largely from integer and address reads rather than reads from floating-point operations. In fact, floating-point operations, including those for read and write operations, remain largely invariant with compiler optimization.

Memory write operations are summarized in Tables 3.30a and b. The VAX values (Table 3.30a) are unnecessarily high because the Fortran compiler generated excessive memory traffic when referencing complex array elements. If the FFT program is excluded from this average then a total value of .35 would result. Write memory traffic for the different architectures was generally the same. As a consequence, the memory traffic per instruction on the more efficient architectures (fewest instructions) is higher. For the least efficient machine, P-code, there are .47 memory references per instruction, but for the VAX architecture there are 1.25 memory references per instruction. Given equal memory systems, a P-code processor would need to be 2.7 times faster than a VAX implementation to execute the composite mix in equal time.

Table 3.30: Memory writes by data type (per CI operation).

(a) Simple

CI		Integer	Real	Other	Total
CI					.33
S/370	Fortran Hopt1	.12	.17	.01	.30
P-Code	Pascal	.22	.12	–	.34
VAX UNIX	Fortran	.40	.23	–	.63
PDP-11	C	.24	.15	–	.40

(b) Optimized

S/370	Fortran Hopt4	.12	.15	.01	.28
VAX/VMS	Fortran	.21	.07	–	.28
HP Precision	Fortran	.12	.18	–	.30

Table 3.31: CI branch statistics.

Program	Unconditional	Conditional		Total
		Taken	Not Taken	
FFT	1,030	7,040	555	8,625
Mort	176,942	463,367	405,142	1,045,451
Norm	1,175	69,071	7,771	78,017
Sort	4,828	111,068	81,042	196,938

Write operations as a class are relatively insensitive to compiler optimizations. Here again, VAX represents the only significant deviation due to the effects of the FFT program.

3.4:   Control

Instruction sequence mechanisms control the flow of instructions to an architecture. Explicit control flow changes result from the execution of branch instructions. Implicit control flow changes result from interrupts or program execution errors; these branches will not be discussed in this study of user state execution. A branch can be unconditional, or conditional on some data event or outcome. Special cases exist where the condition is always false. Instructions of this type are called no-ops. If a condition is true the branch is taken and instruction sequencing continues at the location specified by the instruction. Table 3.31 summarizes the branch behavior specified by the CI measures. The CI measures indicate that 24 percent of the operations are potential branches and, of these, 90 percent are conditional. Of the conditional branches, 66 percent are taken.

Table 3.32: Branch instruction percentages (relative to each machine).

(a) Simple

		FFT	Mort	Norm	Sort	Average
S/370	Fortran Hopt1	5.1	18.0	3.5	14.4	10
P-Code	Pascal	2.0	10.7	2.2	7.8	6
VAX UNIX	Fortran	6.6	31.2	9.0	23.6	18
PDP-11	C	3.5	23.6	4.1	15.1	12

(b) Optimized

		FFT	Mort	Norm	Sort	Average
S/370	Fortran Hopt4	–	–	–	–	14.8
VAX/VMS	Fortran	12.4	–	15.9	29.1	19.1
HP-PA	Fortran	6.5	26.2	8.2	21.4	15.6

Table 3.33: Branches (per thousand CI operations).

(a) Simple

		Unconditional	Conditional		Total
			Taken	Not taken	
CI		23	146	74	243
S/370	Fortran Hopt1	39	145	78	262
P-Code	Pascal	39	145	78	262
VAX	Fortran	56	150	80	286
PDP-11	C	54	150	72	276

(b) Optimized

		Unconditional	Taken	Not taken	Total
S/370	Fortran Hopt4	40	168	55	263
VAX/VMS	Fortran	14	142	56	212
HP Precision	Fortran	31	150	80	261

3.4.1: Branch Instruction Stream

Branches comprise a major portion of the instruction stream. From the CI measures, branches account for 24 percent of the operations. Tables 3.32a and b summarize the branch frequencies for the test set. The branch frequencies are much lower than the CI measures would predict. If absolute counts are examined, then much closer agreement is found. The relative frequencies (per thousand CI operations) for the composite mix are shown in Tables 3.33a and b. The branch instructions are broken down into the same categories used for the CI branch statistics. The conditional breakdowns are nearly identical, while the unconditional branches show some disagreement. In examining the machine code, we found that excess unconditional branches were used to support run-time requirements. These effects are accounted for in the next chapter.

Conditional Branch Invariance

The total number of conditional branches in a program is relatively constant over architecture and level of compiler optimization. The number of branches in a typical architecture follows closely the numbers predicted by our CI measures. Unconditional branches, on the other hand, are more directly affected by both architecture and compilation.

As branches remain constant over levels of optimization and the remaining instructions are reduced by optimization, the net effect is that the relative frequency of branches increases, making the effective branch more important for the machine designer.

Table 3.34: Branch conditions (per thousand CI operations)—simple compilation only.

Condition	S/370 Fortran opt 1	P-Code[1] Pascal	VAX Fortran	PDP-11 C
$\leq$	106	14	33	46
$\neq$	35	23	27	37
$<$	27	23	65	37
$\geq$	23	22	27	59
$=$	36	30	20	
$>$	9	106	47	25

[1]The condition is contained in the compare-for-condition instructions which precede a Boolean conditional branch instruction.

In all cases, the number of conditional branches specified by the high-level-language program (the CI branch measure) are executed by the architecture. Consider now the kind of conditional branch instructions that are executed. The PDP-11, VAX, and S/370 architectures use condition codes that are set by earlier instructions and tested by later branch instructions. Often a branch is preceded by a compare or arithmetic instruction to set the proper codes. S/370 has a special group of branch instructions that perform simple arithmetic and direct the outcome of the branch, but do not affect the condition codes. The VAX has a similar mechanism but changes the condition codes. P-code branch instructions pop the value on the stack and interpret it as a Boolean value. For the P-code machine, only one conditional branch instruction exists (branch on false). Table 3.34 displays the branch conditions used by the composite mix. The results show the wide variability in the conditions tested.

Compiler designers have a certain amount of flexibility when generating loop conditions. For example, moving the test from the beginning

Table 3.35: Instruction break frequency.

(a) Simple

		No Prediction	Detect Unconditionals
S/370	Fortran Hopt1	5.9	4.7
P-Code	Pascal	3.2	2.7
VAX	Fortran	10.3	7.5
PDP-11	C	4.8	4.3

(b) Optimized

S/370	Fortran Hopt4	–	–
VAX/VMS	Fortran	13.8	12.7
HP Precision	Fortran	10.2	8.5

The percent of instruction breaks and the percent of conditional instruction breaks. Thus, the first = unconditional + taken conditional, and the second = taken conditional.

to the end can complement the condition. Also, reversing the operand order inverts the sense of the test. The somewhat uniform distribution of branch conditions would not support implementing special facilities for equal or not equal. An equal comparison is simpler and faster than a signed compare, but for this work load only 7.4 percent of the conditions are of this type.

Branch instructions are a source of pipeline breaks in high performance machines. If a branch is taken, then the normal instruction prefetching and any partial results for later instructions must be aborted. Several techniques exist to predict the outcome of a branch instruction before it can be executed. The simplest mechanism is to assume no branches. When a branch is taken, then a time penalty is incurred. An easy refinement to this approach detects unconditional branches and signals the prefetch unit in time to avoid penalties. Table 3.35 displays the fraction of instructions that causes pipeline delays. For example, 5.9 percent of the Hopt1 instruction stream is a taken branch, but 4.7 percent of that same instruction stream is conditional branches. If the frequency of taken branches is inverted, a measure of the number of instructions executed in a sequence—the run-length—is obtained. Again for the S/370, the run-length is 16.9 instructions, reflecting the scientific work load used in this study. A systems-oriented work load would have a lower value. The distribution of run-lengths is listed in Figure 3.5 and shows the heavy skew to the smaller values. The average value is 17 instructions, but the median value is between 8 and 15 instructions.

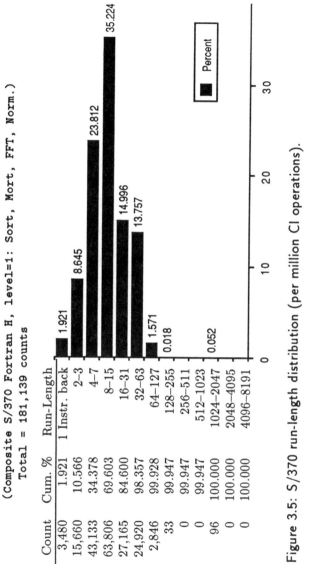

(Composite S/370 Fortran H, level=1: Sort, Mort, FFT, Norm.)
Total = 181,139 counts

Count	Cum. %	Run-Length	Percent
3,480	1.921	1 Instr. back	1.921
15,660	10.566	2–3	8.645
43,133	34.378	4–7	23.812
63,806	69.603	8–15	35.224
27,165	84.600	16–31	14.996
24,920	98.357	32–63	13.757
2,846	99.928	64–127	1.571
33	99.947	128–255	0.018
0	99.947	256–511	
0	99.947	512–1023	
96	100.000	1024–2047	0.052
0	100.000	2048–4095	
0	100.000	4096–8191	

Figure 3.5: S/370 run-length distribution (per million CI operations).

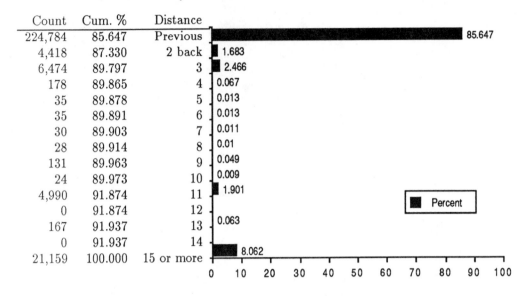

(Composite S/370 Fortran H, level=1: Sort, Mort, FFT, Norm.)
Total = 262,453 counts

Count	Cum. %	Distance
224,784	85.647	Previous
4,418	87.330	2 back
6,474	89.797	3
178	89.865	4
35	89.878	5
35	89.891	6
30	89.903	7
28	89.914	8
131	89.963	9
24	89.973	10
4,990	91.874	11
0	91.874	12
167	91.937	13
0	91.937	14
21,159	100.000	15 or more

Figure 3.6: S/370 branch resolution distance (per million CI operations).

An alternative branch prediction technique can be evaluated by using the collected data. S/370 branch instructions form the target address by adding a base register to a displacement. When the displacement is zero, a short form of the instruction is used. The contents of the base register could have changed in any of the preceding instructions. Therefore, there is an address interlock on the branch's target address. If the branch is conditional, then an additional interlock exists for the condition code values. The S/370 monitor was instrumented to calculate backward the number of instructions to the place all interlocks were resolved. This distance is termed the *branch resolution distance*.

PDP-11 and VAX instructions always set the condition codes. Conditional branches usually have a branch resolution distance of one. Unconditional branch targets can be determined at any point and have an infinite branch resolution distance. Figure 3.6 displays the branch resolution distances for the S/370 architecture. While the architecture allows the setting of condition codes well in advance of their use, there is no indication it is being used. Almost 90 percent of all branches cannot be resolved more than three instructions back and 86 percent of the branches depend on the previous instruction. One reason for these high percentages involves unconditional branches. If the target of a branch cannot be reached by using the 12-bit displacement and the current

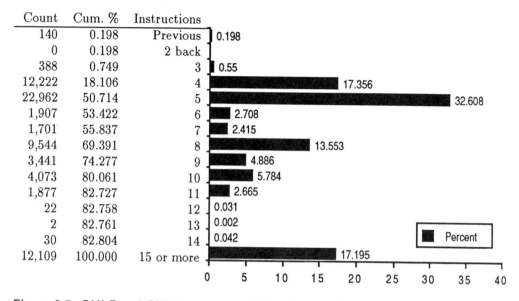

Figure 3.7: BXLE and BXH branch resolution distance (per million CI operations).

base register values, then an extra instruction is inserted to load the correct value into a base register. The added load instruction creates a target address interlock. In Figure 3.6, 14 percent of the branches are unconditional. The obvious solution employed by the VAX and PDP-11 is to use program counter relative addressing for branch targets. In that way all unconditional branches can be resolved at any point in the pipeline.

Figure 3.7 examines the branch resolution distance for specific S/370 instructions. The results are shown for the BXLE and BXH instructions of the composite mix using the Hopt3 compiler. These instructions add a value to a register, compare to another register, and branch if greater than (BXH) or less than or equal (BXLE) to zero. Used in loop control structures, the branch resolution distances are quite large. In pipelines that did not get more than three instructions ahead, 99 percent of these branches could be correctly predicted by using whatever values are in the registers at the time the branch is fetched. These data support the use of instructions that prevent pipeline breaks by signaling special events early in the pipeline. In this example, the condition to be tested is fully specified by the instruction and allows early prediction of the outcome. More sophisticated compiler techniques [30,52] eliminate nearly all of the pipeline breaks due to conditional branching in high-level-language programs.

3.4.2: Branch Distance

The target address of a branch instruction is encoded in many different ways. S/370 adds a 12-bit displacement to a base register to form a branch target address. Software conventions set a base register to the starting location of a procedure at entry time. Branches within 4,096 bytes can be done in one instruction and larger branches require an extra load of the target address. The P-code machine uses an 18-bit field, which spans its whole address space. The PDP-11 and VAX architectures use short displacements for conditional branches and short or long displacements for unconditional branches. The P-code, PDP-11, and VAX architectures use program counter relative addressing to generate the target address. For the VAX and PDP-11, when the displacement field is not large enough to hold the true target, it is necessary to complement the sense of the test and insert a longer unconditional branch. Table 3.36 summarizes the branch direction for the different architectures of all encountered branches. As expected, each architecture branched the same amount in each direction. The roughly 50–50 split in forward and backward branches is similar to results of other studies [48,59]. The symmetric branch direction supports positive and negative displacements, but recall the BXLE and BXH instructions generated by the S/370 Fortran Hopt3 compiler. Since they are used to terminate loop constructs, more than 99 percent are backward branches. The VAX architecture has similar loop constructs (e.g., ACBx, AOBxxx). These instructions use a symmetric offset that halves the backward range of the loop instruction. This illustrates an effort by instruction set designers to assist in machine condition prediction. The PDP-11 architecture has a similar loop instruction (e.g., SOB). But the SOB instruction only branches backward. Symmetric branch ranges are most effective for general purpose branch instructions, but special purpose control structures can exhibit very asymmetrical behavior. By carefully dictating compiler strategies for control structures, specific branch instructions can be forced to go one direction or the other. In one study [66] all conditional branches branched forward to optimize the span of if and while statements.

The distance spanned by a branch is summarized in Figure 3.8. While the S/370 does not use PC-relative branching, the percentages were calculated as if it had half-word (2-byte) offset PC-relative addressing. The PDP-11 curve does not include unconditional branches beyond an

Table 3.36: Branch direction percentages (simple compilation).

		Forward	Backward	Not Taken
S/370	Fortran Hopt1	25	44	31
P-Code	Pascal	25	44	31
VAX	Fortran	29	43	28
PDP-11*	C	33	37	30

* Does not include unconditional branches > ±256 bytes.

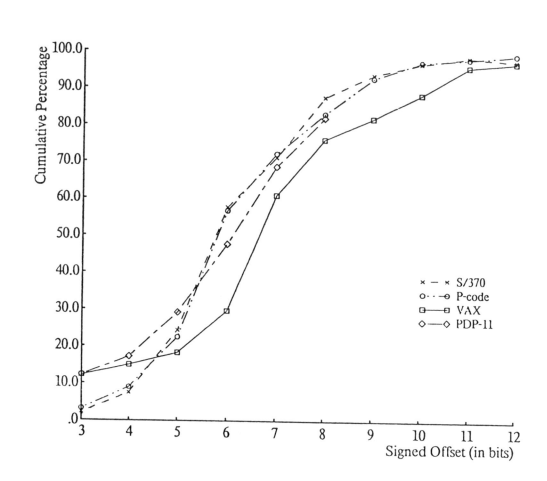

Figure 3.8: Cumulative branch coverage percentage.

8-bit range. There are two major effects evident in this table. The first is the range of the offset in bytes. Since the VAX is a byte addressable instruction stream, an 8-bit offset can only span 256 bytes. The P-code machine is word addressable, so an 8-bit offset spans four times the VAX (1024 bytes). The second effect is the number of instructions from a branch to its target. There are many tradeoffs in determining the addressability of the instruction stream. By allowing greater flexibility, such as in the VAX, a reduced branch span may result.

To better reconcile the values in Figure 3.8, recall from the earlier discussion of program size that the average P-code program is roughly twice the size of a PDP-11, VAX, or S/370 program. If the branch to target span is uniformly distributed throughout a program, then we would expect P-code's 4-byte offset to be twice as effective as the VAX offset. Figure 3.8 confirms this observation, but certain effects may change this relationship.

3.5:   Conclusions

Comparing five architectures and two levels of optimizations shows dramatic differences in the common static and dynamic measures. Each difference is the result of a mixture of factors that must be identified before any conclusions can be drawn. The next chapter discusses the computer optimization factors.

The dramatic 2:1 static size difference between loosely-encoded relatively fixed instruction size architectures (e.g., S/370 and HP-PA) and the highly encoded variable length instruction size architecture (of VAX) is certainly significant. Additional work is needed to completely characterize this difference and to consider alternatives that capture the best aspects of these architectures.

While the importance of static size may be weighted relatively low, the dynamic instruction measures are crucial and show an important tradeoff between absolute count and the interpretive effort necessary for each instruction.

This program set caused RISC type architectures to need 10 percent to 70 percent more instructions and require 25 percent more instruction bandwidth (bytes/task for HP-PA relative to S/370).

The VAX architecture proved most effective when considering only *total instructions*, but examination into the effort necessary to execute the instructions argues for the simpler S/370 or RISC (HP Precision) architecture. The data memory traffic was largely controlled by the number of registers and compiler technology. The design of the instruction set and its efficiency had little effect on this critical measure. The value of registers and the importance of effective register allocation (optimized compiler) is apparent. While effective in reducing the memory traffic, the relative frequency of generalized immediate operands must be re-evaluated in light of modern compiler technology.

The memory referencing requirements made by each architecture are very similar except when superior compilers are used, providing reductions of 50 percent for the S/370 and VAX architectures. The number and extent of mechanisms that address memory operands varied greatly between architectures, but the mechanism most used was the simple base register plus displacement. Different methods to encode the displacement field were compared and an 8-bit displacement proved successful for local variables and arguments. Addressing global objects requires larger displacements and may perhaps require a totally different mechanism to be effective.

ANALYZING COMPUTER ARCHITECTURES

Chapter 4

Compiler Effects on Instruction
Execution

CHAPTER 4. COMPILER EFFECTS

Chapter 4: Compiler Effects on Instruction Execution

4.1: Introduction

This study of computer instruction sets is concerned with both time and space minimization of executed programs. The various strategies and techniques used by the compiler to generate machine code (the code generator) make differing use of the machine's instruction set. Given a specific program and machine, two distinct compilers produce different machine code. These differences change many important measures of instruction set effectiveness.

For example, Table 4.1 shows the instruction count and main memory read activity for an integer Sort program. The program was compiled for the IBM S/370 computer by using the enhanced Fortran H compiler. The first column shows the two measures with no optimization, and the second with full optimization. In this example, the machine remains the same and the dramatic reduction in these measures is due entirely to the compiler. By contrast, the UNIX Fortran compiler produced VAX 11/780 code that executed fewer instructions (925,113), but more memory reads (824,856) for the same Sort program. These measures include both compiler and architecture effects and do not allow immediate architectural comparisons.

In this chapter, the relationship between the compiler and the instruction set is analyzed by examining compiled program execution on a fixed architecture. Differences in a program's representation and changes in the instruction stream due to the compiler are termed *compiler effects*. A more optimized program presumably executes fewer instructions and makes smaller demands on the resources of the ma-

Table 4.1: Sort program execution measures.

Measure	IBM S/370 Fortran H Compiler	
	No Optimization	Full Optimization
Instructions Executed	2,148,680	1,131,865
Memory Reads	1,347,586	291,943

chine. Compiler effects are categorized by the source of these differences or changes. The first category, *invariants*, groups those aspects of the instruction stream that are not affected by the compiler. Measures of these effects remain the same.

The semantics of high-level languages influence the optimality of compiled code. The language itself is the source of instruction set measurement differences. This second category, *language effects*, has prompted people to consider machines dedicated to a single language [10].

Machine-independent effects reflect optimizations by the compiler that do not depend on the image machine. A fair comparison of architectures must first filter these effects from the analysis. Machine-independent optimizations include some code motion, some common subexpression elimination, and some induction variable elimination. These optimizations are by definition applicable to a wide variety of architectures. They are often coupled with other types of optimizations to provide the greatest performance gains.

Machine-dependent effects require that the compiler understand more about the architecture. The allocation of variables to registers is an optimization based on the architecture. It is important to include these effects in the analysis to avoid an unfair handicap to machines without sophisticated compilers. Computer designers can control the extent to which optimization applies to an instruction set by selecting features complementary to current compiler techniques.

This study examines Fortran and Pascal programs compiled for the IBM S/370 architecture. There are three distinct compilers and four levels of optimization for one of the compilers, providing six compilation strategies.

4.2: Invariant Effects

Compiler strategies and optimization techniques do not always produce different or better machine code. There are certain high-level-language constructs that produce unvarying code sequences.

4.2.1: *Highly Specialized Constructs*

Input/output (I/O) is a highly specialized high-level-language construct. In nearly all cases, I/O is supported by a fixed set of carefully coded routines. Optimization techniques do not affect the frequency or duration of these I/O operations, and the mapping from the high-level-language source program to the machine code is largely one-to-one. In some architectures, highly specialized instructions provide an exact surrogate for a high-level-language construct. The P-code machine has the

> Compiler Effects
>
> The influence of the compiler on the instruction stream is profound. It is often much larger than the underlying architectural differences themselves and totally confounds any measures of architectural effectiveness. The sources of these influences are:
>
> - Invariants.
>
> - Language effects.
>
> - Machine-independent effects.
>
> - Machine-dependent effects.
>
> Each provides information to better analyze measurements of program execution. In some cases, measurements can be directly used (as in conditional branches), while other measures (such as instruction counts) require a great deal of analysis to make even simple observations. Results of the previous chapter were carefully drawn and include the language effects.
>
> The discussion in Section 4.2 organizes compilation and optimization in categories that distinguish its effect on the instruction stream. This sets a framework to analyze the data to separate architectural differences from compiler and language differences.
>
> Traditional benchmarking techniques report only total time or a similar measure. Instead, architecture comparison should include compiler and language effects in the analysis to draw even the simplest conclusions.

trigonometric functions as operations, so the existence of a **sin** call in the P-code machine's high-level language, Pascal, always results in a **sin** operation in the machine code.

The inclusion or exclusion of highly specialized instructions can be evaluated by the instruction set designer. The absolute occurrence of specialized constructs is invariant to compiler technology; however, better optimization of other, more common constructs increases their relative frequency. Highly specialized functions could be part of a common subexpression, but this possibility is considered small and is treated later. Table 4.2 lists the absolute number of highly specialized operands used by the P-code machine for the execution of the four test programs. They include I/O, trigonometric functions, and other predefined functions (ex., **abs, sqrt**). The CI operation measure is used to scale each entry. This results in a relative frequency of four specialized instructions per thousand CI operations. With this information along with specific knowledge of anticipated workloads an instruction set designer

Table 4.2: P-code specialized instruction counts (totals).

Program	Specialized Instructions
FFT	26
Mort	323
Norm	9793
Sort	none

can make design tradeoffs. For this example, the allocation of the standard opcode space (those opcodes that are most easily decoded) to the trigonometric functions and I/O primitives is not warranted.

In the P-code machine the standard procedures are grouped into a single escape opcode that uses an operand specification field to indicate the functions. Since these specialized instructions normally require greater amounts of interpretation time anyway, the small additional decode time is justified.

4.2.2: Floating point

Other operations that are less specialized are also largely invariant with compiler effects. Floating-point operations fall into this category. Table 4.3 lists the several different kinds of floating operations for the six S/370 compilers and levels. The counts are similar, since they reflect a strategy common to all S/370 compilers for built-in Fortran functions (e.g., floating absolute value). While the machine must perform the indicated function (whether in-line expanded or linked to a subroutine package), there are only a few optimization techniques that could reduce the number of executed floating-point instructions. The first, *early-out* expression evaluation, takes advantage of Boolean identity functions to shortcut a Boolean expression's evaluation. In this set of benchmarks, early-out optimization involving floating point occurred in one statement.

The second floating-point optimization technique eliminates evaluation of common subexpressions. The FFT program, by design, allows very little optimization. For the Norm program, which makes the most use of floating-point constructs, the largest change in the total number of executed floating-point operations was seven percent. Norm contains long sequences of assignment statements, yet little reduction occurred.

The algorithms employed in the Norm program were designed to minimize floating-point operations. It is likely that programmers are more acutely aware of potential floating-point penalties, and design source programs accordingly. Table 4.4 shows the breakdown of the various

Table 4.3: S/370 floating-point operation frequency (average per thousand CI operations).

S/370		Add/Sub	Multiply	Divide
	G	146	105	6.9
	Hopt0	148	105	6.9
Fortran	Hopt1	135	105	6.9
	Hopt2	130	104	6.9
	Hopt3	130	104	6.9
Pascal/VS		154	105	6.9

Table 4.4: S/370 Norm floating-point statement types (totals in thousands).

S/370		Add/Sub		Multiply		Divide		Totals
		RR	RX	RR	RX	RR	RX	
	G	45	126	17	126	–	11	324
	Hopt0	15	161	–	143	–	11	329
Fortran	Hopt1	82	86	32	111	3.1	7.6	322
	Hopt2	49	108	22	118	3.1	7.6	307
	Hopt3	49	108	22	118	3.1	7.6	307
Pascal/VS		42	123	19	124	3.2	7.4	321

floating-point operations by S/370 statement type. RR-type instructions operate on data operands in registers and RX type instructions fetch one operand from main memory, while the other operand and destination is a register. Table 4.4 shows that each compiler and level generates very different instructions yet the total number of operations stays constant. The effect of optimization is largely reflected in the number of loads. Table 4.5 shows the poor performance of the H level 0 compiler and the otherwise steady improvement. The number of stores is a direct reflection of assignment statements and remains quite constant (within 5 percent), apart from the Hopt0 compiler anomaly.

Several other machines executed the Norm program, and the strategy used for the code generation of built-in functions affects their results. Since there are no standard functions used by the Norm program with implied multiplies or divides, these values can be accurately compared. Table 4.6 shows the number of floating-point multiplies and divides executed on each of the machines for the Norm program. Again, the absolute occurrence remains constant. In examining the code generated by each compiler, we find the only source of difference occurs in code generation for mixed-mode expressions. The C compiler takes the most efficient course by using integer arithmetic as long as possible in expression evaluation.

Table 4.5: S/370 Norm floating-point memory references (totals in thousands).

S/370		Fetches	Stores
Fortran	G	437	133
	Hopt0	651	336
	Hopt1	430	137
	Hopt2	345	130
	Hopt3	345	130
Pascal/VS		405	132

Table 4.6: Norm floating-point operations (totals in thousands).

		Add/Sub	Multiply	Divide
CI		143	133	10.6
P-Code	Pascal	143	142	10.7
VAX	Fortran	141	142	10.7

The four test programs on the S/370 individually exhibit relative floating-point operation frequencies of 0 to 38 percent, and the CI weighted averages range from 4.0 percent to 9.6 percent. The S/370 architecture allocates 51 opcodes for 19.9 percent of the basic opcode set to floating-point operations. All of the 51 opcodes use RR and RX type formats. Suppose we consider one simple recoding of the instruction set and examine the costs. The use of an escape opcode is a common technique to extend a machine's opcode space. It is similar to Foster's conditional opcodes [24], except the duration of the conditional evaluation is one instruction. The S/370 architecture uses instructions that are 2, 4, or 6 bytes long. To stay within that framework, we define six opcodes from the basic opcode set as *floating-point opcodes*. The first four are the standard load and store of short and long operands. The last two are used as an escape to RR type and RX type floating-point operations. A floating-point instruction is reencoded by simply replacing the original opcode with the appropriate RR or RX escape opcode and appending a 16-bit operation code to the end of the new instruction.

The hardware difference is insignificant since all of the register specifications and address description fields remain unchanged. A 16-bit operation field is used to prevent an odd instruction length. The cost of this scheme is two bytes for every floating-point operation (except load/store). Overall, the number of instruction bytes fetched would increase in the worst case by 5.3 percent. Even the worst-case increase (Norm Hopt3) would be only 21.2 percent. This scheme frees up 17

> **Average per Thousand CI Operations**
>
> Tables use scaled numbers and averages to summarize the many data points that are collected. The phrase "average per thousand CI operations" is computed, say for some measure x, as the straight average of
>
> $$\frac{\text{total \# of } x \text{ in FFT}}{\text{CI operations in FFT}}, \frac{\text{total \# of } x \text{ in Mort}}{\text{CI operations in Mort}},$$
>
> $$\frac{\text{total \# of } x \text{ in Norm}}{\text{CI operations in Norm}}, \frac{\text{total \# of } x \text{ in Sort}}{\text{CI operations in Sort}}$$
>
> and then scaled by 1,000.
>
> This method of displaying data attempts to equally weight each program's contribution to the final value. This approach will highlight large deviations from the CI measures but can obscure significant differences when the variance on the data points becomes large. All of these issues must be kept in mind when interpreting data.

percent of the basic opcode set and these opcodes could be used to better encode more frequent instructions or make for a shorter major opcode specifier.

The invariance of floating-point operations with compiler effects could be expected. In most traditional architectures there exists a close match between high-level-language semantics and machine-level instructions for floating point. Only by including some highly specialized functions such as SIN or FFT could the number of floating-point instructions be decreased. But even with a reduced number of instructions, a machine executes the same total number of operations with its floating-point unit (whether hardware or firmware). For example, a SIN instruction will not reduce the number of multiplies needed to evaluate it; it will only reduce the number of instructions fetched. The close match between high-level-language semantics and machine-level instructions is largely due to the simplicity of floating point. Architectures need only provide primitive operations (add, sub, mul, div, compare) to assure compiler invariance.

4.2.3: *Control*

High-level-language constructs that direct the sequencing of statements executed are called *control structures*. They can be categorized as either conditional or unconditional. Conditional structures include IF statements and iterative statements. Unconditional structures include GOTO's and procedure calls. Compiler organization and optimizations can rarely reduce the number of conditional and unconditional control

Table 4.7: CI and S/370 conditional branches (totals).

		FFT	Mort	Norm	Sort
CI		7,595	868,509	76,842	192,110
	G	8,107	1,013,270	100,212	192,110
S/370	Hopt0	7,601	886,046	79,899	192,110
Fortran	Hopt1	7,601	886,046	79,899	192,110
	Hopt2	7,601	886,046	79,899	192,110
	Hopt3	7,601	886,046	79,899	192,110
S/370 Pascal/VS		7,595	887,355	78,183	192,110

transfers specified by a program. We first examine the invariant aspects of control structures, and later the exceptions that can reduce the control transfer counts.

Branches

The existence of a conditional control transfer in the high-level-language program maps directly to an equivalent machine instruction sequence. The method used to evaluate Boolean expressions may vary but the execution of the corresponding conditional branch or skip instruction is a direct result of the high-level-language control construct. On the other hand, it is possible for a compiler to generate implied conditional operations, such as bounds checks, that may need to be accounted for separately. Table 4.7 shows the number of executed conditional branches for the four programs. The almost identical counts indicate how strong this invariance is for the S/370 compilers. There are a few exceptions. Early-out evaluation could result in extra conditional branches, but the frequency of long Boolean expressions that allow early-out evaluation is small. The S/370 Fortran G compiler counts need to be adjusted for two run-time effects. Conversion from fixed point to floating point (implicit or explicit) is done without branch instructions by the H compiler, while the G compiler generates a conditional branch. This explains most of the differences in the counts for the FFT and Norm programs. Additionally, the Fortran G compiler generates in-line code for implied DO loops used in I/O statements. Nearly all the differences for the Mort program can be traced to this effect. Run-time environments can dramatically affect instruction set information.

As in the case of floating point, the absolute occurrence of conditional control transfers is nearly invariant with the compiler. From Table 4.7, the CI values represent between 12 percent and 32 percent of the total

Table 4.8: Conditional branches (averages per CI operation).

		Conditional Branches
CI		.220
S/370	Fortran Hopt3	.223
VAX	Fortran	.230
PDP-11	C	.223

CI operations specified (average = 22 percent) and thereby comprise a significant portion of all executed operations. The conditional branch results for each of the machines is shown in Table 4.8. Not only are conditional branches invariant with compiler effects, but they remain constant for all architectures.

Unconditional control transfers are not nearly so invariant. Here the compiler effects measurements of instruction set execution. Again, the run-time environment contributes greatly to the varying statistics. For example, the S/370 Fortran linkage convention includes several unconditional transfers as the result of programming conventions. The Fortran G compiler generates four unconditional branches for each procedure call. None are necessary. Instructions are laid out in main memory in the following order: entry, name, linkage, static variables, prologue, epilogue, and main body. An ordering: name, entry, linkage, prologue, main body, epilogue, and static variable, would eliminate each unconditional branch. The Fortran H compiler organizes a subroutine: entry, name, linkage, static variables, body, epilogue, and prologue. This again forces four unneeded branches and the code could be reordered to exclude these branches.

Evaluation of built-in functions by separate procedures contributes to the high number of subroutine calls in the two programs with floating point. It is reasonable to expect any machine to execute the same number of subroutine calls as indicated by the CI environment measure. One exception is compiler designs, which expand in-line explicit user procedures to reduce call frequencies. One strategy is to expand all leaf procedures (a procedure that makes no calls to any other procedures). For most cases, a space–time tradeoff must be considered.

Procedure Calls

For many effects, compiler invariance also implies programmer invariance. Given an algorithm, any program generally executes the same number of floating-point multiplies. Input/output is similar. But for certain control transfers, such as call frequency, source usage is a direct result of the programmer's style.

For our sample test set of programs written in Fortran, the static call frequency is about 6.7 percent and the dynamic call frequency about .3 percent. Many studies of program behavior have examined call frequencies and the overhead associated with the call mechanism. The dynamic Whetstone call frequency was 1.9 percent and the static frequency was 4.6 percent [71]. There are several Whetstone instructions that are used for procedure entry and exit, and sum to a dynamic overhead of about 11 percent. A large percentage of these instructions deals with the checking and copying of actual parameters. The average procedure required 1.8 parameters.

The frequency of call statements in the static source language shows a higher frequency. Table 4.9 gives the static frequency of call statements from several different studies. In most cases the call frequency was quite low, largely reflecting the programmer's choice. More sophisticated programmers [3,63,66] use call statements more frequently. Table 4.10 lists the static and dynamic frequencies for several studies of languages and machines. From the instruction set designer's perspective, the call frequency is a very important parameter. However, static frequencies are very poor indicators of the dynamic values, and indicate call statements are less frequently used than their appearance in the program indicates.

Structured programming techniques increasing the modularity in programs may produce more procedure calls. Two studies of the UNIX environment [48,50] show dynamic Call statement frequencies of 4.69 percent and 12 percent, respectively.

While the frequency of Call statements diminishes when programs are executed, the complexity of a Call operation underscores its importance. In one PDP-11 study [48], the Call frequency was only 3.7 percent, yet the overhead to save the processor state and perform the linkage accounted for over one-fifth of all instructions executed. Instruction set designers can expect the Call frequency to increase due to structured programming techniques. Only through in-line expansion of user procedures can compiler optimization techniques reduce Call frequencies.

4.3:   Language Effects

4.3.1:   Variable Referencing

The programming language itself may affect the use of a computer instruction set. Given the same machine, the same algorithm, but two

Table 4.9: High-level-language static call frequency.

Study	Language	Work Load	Static Calls
Knuth 71	Fortran	Scientific	8%
Knuth 71	Fortran	Student	5%
Robinson 76	Fortran	Scientific	3.2%
Tanenbaum 78	SAL	Compilers/OS	24.6%
Sweet 76	Mesa	Compiler/OS	33.8%
Wortman 72	Student/PL	Student	2.7%
Alexander 72	XPL	Student Compiler/Compiler	13%
Elshoff	PL/I	Commercial	2%

Table 4.10: Static and dynamic call frequency.

Study	Language	Machine	Work Load	Call Frequency	
				Static:	Dynamic:
Knuth 71	Fortran	S/370	Student	5	3
Shustek 78	Fortran PL/I	S/370	System/Scientific	2.6	.4
Shustek 78	Assembler	8080	Graphics	6.1	3.8
Wortman 72	Student/PL Machine	Student/PL	Student	7.6	5.6
Alexander 72	XPL	S/370	Compilers	6.5	1.5
Wichmann 70	Algol	Whetstone	Scientific	4.6	1.9
Neuhauser 79	C	PDP-11	System	10.9	4.3

Invariants

Compiler invariants are the baseline measures that are first reconciled in any architectural comparison. If any differences are observed, one must establish blame or credit for that difference. Round up the usual suspects! Often the run-time environment is to blame. One compiler generated a procedure call to evaluate the complex conjugate function in the FFT program. Another compiler expanded the multiplication of real times complex into a conversion to complex and then multiplied complex times complex.

In most cases, differences in invariant measures are traced to software policies, but occasionally an architectural difference is exposed. Given equivalent software organization, the number of unconditional branches is roughly invariant. The primary perturbation to that invariance is the span or distance of a branch instruction. In the case study section, the VAX approach shows the consequences of the architectural branch span decision.

Another significant characteristic of invariants is that their relative importance (frequency) in the instruction stream increases as higher levels of optimization occur. Optimization removes the other instructions; invariants like branch and floating operations remain. The degree of concurrency and fundamental limits to program execution are determined by the occurrence of, and dependencies among, invariants.

different languages, instruction set measurements can differ greatly. One major source of such differences is variable referencing. In Fortran, for example, actual parameters are normally passed by reference, while Pascal allows a potentially more efficient call-by-value mechanism. The Fortran parameter-passing structure is quite complex and general. Since separately compiled modules are allowed, the most general parameter passing mechanism is always employed. Fortran allows a variable number of arguments for the same procedure. Parameter referencing is most often implemented with tables of indirect access to arguments (even to a parameter such as the constant 1).

Consider simple variables. The Fortran calling semantics require that any assignment to formal parameters must be reflected in the actual parameter upon return. Two common mechanisms are used to implement the call. The *copy-in-copy-out* copies each argument's value, as pointed to by the parameter list, to an area local to the procedure (used by S/370 Fortran G and H). Further references to an argument use this local copy. At procedure exit time, the local copies are moved back to the original location. Each reference, within the procedure, uses the local copy. Another mechanism (used by VAX Fortran) uses an argument address list passed on the stack without copying the values to locals—call-by-reference. Each reference within the procedure indirectly accesses the variable through the argument list. For the first case, the number of memory read and write references made to simple arguments is the sum of:

$2 \times$ (simple arguments passed: for copy-in)
$+ 2 \times$ (simple arguments passed: for copy-out)
$+$ (simple arguments passed: for address references during copy-in)
$+$ (simple arguments passed: for address references during copy-out)
$+$ (simple argument references)

while for the latter method the memory reference count is:

(simple argument references)
$+$ (simple argument references: for indirect pointer)

This assumes local simple variables can be referenced without added memory accesses for address computation.

Now consider an algorithm written in Pascal where simple variables can be passed by value. Then the number of simple argument memory references is:

$2 \times$ (simple arguments passed: for copy-in)
$+$ (simple arguments references)

Therefore call-by-value is better than the indirect argument lists when

$2 \times$ (simple arguments passed) $+$ simple argument references

is less than

$2 \times$ (simple arguments references)

and call-by-value is always better than the copy-in–copy-out mechanism. In this study, there were 42,810 memory references for the call-by-value mechanism and 48,320 memory references for the indirect call-by-reference technique. It is assumed that the indirect parameter table is statically allocated and initialized. For recursive languages, additional references would be needed to build the parameters' address list. The break-even point occurs when each passed parameter is referenced twice. If references to generate an address list are included, the break-even point becomes one reference per passed parameter. In this study, each translation tried to preserve the Fortran call mechanism by forcing the explicit use of call-by-reference. The instruction set measurements for this environment make greater use of indirect accesses due to this language effect.

Structured parameters are often passed by reference in languages like Fortran, Pascal and PL/I. The semantics used to calculate the object referenced by a structured access depends on the language and run-time environment. For example, the language C assumes all arrays begin with index 0; the array access uses the exact base address of the array at all times. Fortran assumes arrays are indexed beginning at one. The S/370 Fortran compiler creates two versions of the array's address: the true address, used when passed to subroutines, and a biased address, used to provide direct indexing. For a language like Pascal, which allows arbitrary bounds, additional computation may be necessary. This language effect is most easily compensated for by creating biased pointers. The P-code compiler does not provide this capability, so the opcode distribution includes 12 percent DEC (decrease by constant) instructions to adjust array addresses. The frequency at which biased addresses are created must be weighed against the number of times used. For this study's test set, array indexing far exceeds the overhead to create a biased address. The VAX data indicate that there would be at most a three percent instruction overhead to create biased addresses, and that at least ten percent of the operands were array accesses (as indicated by the index operand mode). Another study [50] found that an average of 25 percent of the variable references accessed arrays or structures. These data show that a specialized index operation, which included a starting index for every array access, would create many more references than biased array bases. This assumes that the starting index is also a reference.

The allocation strategy for variables specified by the language greatly affects the use of an instruction set. Static allocation, as with Fortran, allows the use of immediate addresses that require less computation than base + displacement calculations. S/370 Fortran dedicates base registers to access global (COMMON) and local variables, but if the S/370 architecture provided direct addressing, static allocation could have been used. Pascal allows static allocation of global variables, but all local variables must be referenced through the local frame.

While many techniques exist to efficiently encode dynamic variable references, there will still be a significant change in the computational requirements of the instruction stream due to the language's specification of argument semantics.

4.3.2: Data Types and Structures

The use of an instruction stream is also influenced by the variety of data types allowed. Originally Fortran IV allowed only logical, integer, real, and complex data types. Programs with character processing requirements were forced to circumvent Fortran restrictions by mapping characters into integers. The Mort program references characters almost exclusively, yet the character instructions of the S/370 are unused. In Mort, the programmer stored single characters in 32-bit integers, while mixing array indices and characters in the same array. The program's execution required that characters read in an "A1" format were always numerically greater than an array index. Had the programmer been able to use character data types, the instruction stream would have been very different. Needless to say, this program did not port to the VAX architecture without great effort.

Structured operations are language constructs that greatly affect instruction set use. In the FFT program, an array is copied to another array. Fortran requires a DO loop, while Pascal can use a single assignment statement. String operations are similar. It is very difficult for a compiler to detect that a loop is really a structured assignment. The increasing use of Pascal and other similar languages will change the instruction stream use. In the S/370 emulation, the MOVE LONG instruction was unneeded until Pascal programs were executed. The frequency of instructions like MOVE LONG may be low, but the memory referencing involved can be very high. For the FFT program, if the DO loop used to copy an array were replaced for the S/370 Fortran Hopt3 code with a MOVE LONG instruction, then 20,000 of 118,000 instructions would be saved. However, 16,000 of 76,000 main memory references would result from executing the MOVE LONG 16 times.

To illustrate this language effect further, consider the following program fragments in Fortran and Pascal, respectively:

```
DIMENSION ITEM(100,5)          Item : array[1..100] of record
          .                             Key : integer;
          .                             Field2 : ... end;
          .
     DO 10 J=1,5                          .
10 ITEM(I,J) = ITEM(K,J)                  .
                                          .
                               Item[i] := Item[k];
```

These fragments could be part of a Sort program that copied one object to another. In the Fortran fragment an object corresponds to the row of an array and in Pascal an object is a record element of the array. A Pascal compiler could optimize the structured assignment in many ways since all the record elements are contiguous. Fortran dictates array storage in main memory to be column major, so the row elements being moved by the DO loop are not contiguous. If the compiler tried to optimize DO loops with constant indices for this example, little improvement could be realized. Any good Fortran programmer would have reordered the array indices to be efficient, but not all examples can be so easily improved. For example, parallel arrays are regularly used to simulate a structure when the elements are not the same type.

Language Effects

While language effects did not play a significant role in this analysis, they can be the most critical factor in comparisons. Whenever a language difference is part of an experiment, the analysis must begin with a thorough review of how the programs were generated.

A more recent topic in compiler optimization is "aliasing." This analysis informs the optimizer of the potential for conflicts between variables (and the need to synchronize variable changes through main memory). The semantics, and to a degree the syntax, of the language has a profound influence on the success of an optimizer to avoid extraneous memory loads and stores. Some optimizers violate (without warning) certain semantics of the language to generate more efficient, and potentially incorrect, code.

Global flow analysis can be more effectively applied to languages that restrict the lifetimes of variables. In Pascal, the value of a **for** loop control variable need not be maintained for use outside the loop. The C language requires that the control variable must hold its last value after exit from the loop. This language effect can be very strong in programs that loop repeatedly. For the test set of programs, the S/370 Fortran execution updated loop variables at least 3.8 percent of the time. The VAX Fortran execution updated loop variables at least 3.0 percent of the time. Compilers can optimize the use of control variables for register machines, but will need extra instructions at loop exit to save values.

In all of the test programs, great care was taken to avoid language effects when the original Fortran was translated to Pascal and C. Array bounds in Pascal were declared to begin at one. C does not allow lower bound declarations. No structured operations were included in the Pascal translations. Each machine used similar mechanisms to reference arguments and variables. The major language effect is found in the procedure call mechanism. The VAX, PDP-11, and P-code machines supported recursive calls, while the S/370 Fortran environment did not. Because of the way the programs were translated, language effects can be largely ignored for data from our test set of programs.

4.4: Machine Independent Effects

Optimization performed by a compiler can sometimes be applied to many different representations of a program. These optimizations affect the resulting instruction stream in many different ways. The changes due to optimizations of this type are termed *machine independent effects*. A simple example is found in the following program fragment:

```
    DO 10 I=1,N
        DO 10 J=1,M
10          SUM = SUM + A(I)*B(I,J)
```

The array element A(I) does not change during the execution of the inner loop, and its evaluation could be pulled out of the loop. This type of optimization, *loop invariant code motion*, applies to any architecture to reduce the number of address calculations. The net effect on the instruction stream will depend on the cost of array address calculations.

Machine-independent optimization techniques are described in the following sections. They are included to assist readers of this book in the basic techniques and terminology used by optimizing compilers. An important aspect of this discussion is the identification of the types of changes to the instruction stream that are made by the compiler. For example, some optimizations may not reduce the number of executed instructions, but may simplify the computational demands. Detailed presentation of these techniques can be found in most basic compiler books [2].

4.4.1: Code Motion

Code motion is a general category of optimization techniques which move the execution of code sequences to eliminate either redundant calculations or replications. In the process, temporary names may be introduced to store intermediate values. For optimizations of redundant calculations, the number of executed instructions are smaller but there is usually no change in the static size of the program. In some cases the size increases due to the need to reference the intermediate values. The decreased number of calculations occurs for specific types of computations. Address arithmetic is one of the most common. For the example at the beginning of this section, the calculation of A(I) and the partial calculation of B(I,J) could be moved outside of the inner loop. S/370 Fortran performs address calculations by first multiplying the index by the element size and then by using the base plus index addressing mode to reference the object. For the test work load, nearly all of the index multipliers were powers of two and converted to shift operations. The frequency of shift operations dramatically decreased as greater optimization is used.

The machine-independent effect of code motion is to reduce the number of calculations performed. The number of variables referenced could go up or down, depending on the loop iteration frequency and the complexity of the calculation. To achieve the greatest performance gain, code motion is coupled with optimizations that allocate fast storage locations and short names to these intermediate values.

Replicated code occurs when two different paths of a program have a common code sequence and a single copy of the code can precede the separate paths. No savings in dynamic execution time is found, but a reduced static program size is achieved. Another optimization does not move code but rather branches from the redundant code segment to save space. In this instance an additional branch is executed and the space–time tradeoff must be closely examined.

4.4.2: Common Subexpressions

Common subexpression elimination is an optimization technique that replaces already-computed code sequences with a reference to the named result. Both the static size and dynamic number of executed instructions are reduced. As was true for code motion, the eliminated instructions computed expressions. They could be address calculations, fixed-point arithmetic, or floating-point values. The savings in variable references depend on the complexity of the common expressions and the frequency of use. For example, consider the program fragment:

$$\vdots$$

$$A := (B + C) * (C + E);$$
$$F := (B + C) * G;$$

$$\vdots$$

The common subexpression computation "$B + C$" requires two references and an add operation. If not optimized, four references and two adds are required. When optimized, two references are needed to create the intermediate value and to retrieve it in the second statement. But two references and the add are eliminated. While this is not a large savings, if A and B were complex variables, the savings would be more dramatic. As with the code motion optimization, the larger payoff results when this optimization is coupled with register allocation or other high-speed storage allocation techniques.

4.4.3: Strength Reduction

Strength reduction replaces a relatively expensive (in time or space) operation with a cheaper one. The most common example occurs during array indexing. To calculate an array address, the index is multiplied by the element size and is added to the array base. Often the element size is a power of two and is more simply calculated as a shift operation. Strength reduction is a machine-independent effect in the sense that most machines provide simple primitives before more complex operations. There are exceptions; the P-code machine provides integer multiply but doesn't have shift operators. A special instruction was created to perform efficient array indexing.

Other examples replace **mod** operators with masking and replace divide operations with right shifts. In each case, the number of instructions is not changed nor is the number of variable references. What does change is the actual operation. The speedup due to these optimizations depends on the implementation. There is another group of strength reductions which produces far greater savings. Aho and Ullman [2] give a dramatic example from PL/I, where:

$$L = \text{LENGTH}(S1||S2)$$

is reduced to:

$$L = \text{LENGTH}(S1) + \text{LENGTH}(S2)$$

In this example, the string concatenation ("||") is avoided by applying the identity: the length of concatenated strings is the sum of the lengths of each string. Similar reductions in arithmetic expressions are possible. In these later examples the number of executed instructions as well as the number of variable references is reduced.

4.4.4: *Special Constructs*

High-level languages provide programmers with general constructs. In some instances, very specific use of a construct may need only a small part of the generality allowed. For these cases, optimizations can significantly improve the performance of the program. To illustrate, the Pascal function call is a general procedure call that returns a result. When a very special instance of that structure is used, a very different code sequence may be possible. The IBM 801 compiler expands simple leaf procedures as a macro [7]. A leaf procedure makes no calls of its own. The general call mechanism is circumvented by reorganizing a special construct. This is a time optimization, and the static size of a program will increase if more than one call to the leaf procedure exists.

The dynamic instruction stream is affected with this construct in a manner very different from other machine independent effects. Computation requirements are the same, but the control and linkage instructions to implement the call are eliminated. This includes two unconditional branches and several variable references for argument passing. It may be necessary to make copies of value parameters, but in all cases the optimization reduces the number of executed instructions. The frequency of leaf procedure calls cannot be determined from the data collected, so an estimate of the magnitude of this effect cannot be made.

Built-in functions are similar in many respects to the leaf procedures just discussed. The CI measure assumes that the operation exists, but it may require several instructions to implement on a given architecture. The dynamic instruction stream may either compute the function in-line or branch to a subroutine that performs that function. The tradeoffs are similar to those in the leaf procedure discussion. The frequency of built-in functions in the test work load is less than one percent. Their effects are quite small and are discussed in later sections.

Other examples of special constructs include special call sequences for non-recursive or very simple procedures. In **case** statements, different methods of determining the jump address can be optimized to the number and kinds of cases found, eliminating excess instructions. The compilers in this study do not perform these optimizations, thus simplifying the analysis.

4.4.5: Induction Variables

Induction variable elimination is an optimization that simplifies loop iterations. If the value of one variable can be inferred from the value of another, then it is possible to eliminate one name and replace it with an expression in terms of the other variable. For example, consider a simple loop to duplicate a complex array:

```
DO 10 I =1,100
10      A(I) = B(I)
```

The address calculation introduces an intermediate value (for, say, an S/370):

$$T = I * 16$$

T and I are induction variables where T could be initialized to 16 and incremented by 16 each time through the loop. The test to terminate the loop could compare against 1600 and thereby eliminate any need to calculate $I * 16$ or reference I.

Induction variable elimination reduces both the size of a program and the number of executed instructions. As was the case with code motion and common subexpressions, computational instructions are eliminated; the necessary control instructions remain. The distribution of constants needed by the instruction stream changes. What was originally an increment by "1" operation now requires loop iterations to jump by the size of the array element. Studies that examined loop behavior [39,66] report a very high fraction of loops that increment the control variable by one. The need for a special increment instruction must be re-evaluated in light of advances in compiler technology. Data in the last chapter showed that a very simple optimization of array indices reduced references to the constants zero and one from 41 percent to 20 percent of immediate operands.

Induction variables also reduce the number of names that need to be addressed, while many other optimization techniques introduce new variables. Often termed *compiler created variables* (CCV's), new names increase the demands and potentially reduce the effectiveness of architectural features such as registers. Some architectures have provided automatic mechanisms to index commonly used array sizes to circumvent the problem from the beginning. The VAX offers an addressing mode that scales the index by the value 1, 2, 4, or 8 for address generation. There is no need to create intermediate names or include explicit instructions to perform the calculation. It is still necessary to perform the scaling operation and that cost must be evaluated.

4.4.6:   Other Optimizations

There are other machine-independent optimizations that can be done; *loop unrolling* and *loop jamming* result in the same number of calculations but reduce the number of control tests needed by the loop structure. Neither of these techniques is used by compilers in this study.

Generally, machine-independent compiler optimizations reduce the computational requirements of a program. In some cases control points are reduced or eliminated. The compiler invariant conditional branches can be compromised by using leaf procedure expansion, loop unrolling, and loop jamming. Architectural studies that include compilers with these capabilities must adjust the results to reflect these differences.

4.5:   Machine Dependent Effects

There are many instances where the compiler may take advantage of an architecture. A machine-dependent effect results from optimizations that apply in different ways to different machines. For example, strength reduction described in the previous section applies to fixed-point computations. The S/370 architecture provides a **halve** instruction for floating-point operands. Optimizing a "divide by two" into

Machine Independent Effects

Machine-independent effects are the most important effects that must
be accounted for in making architectural comparisons. One wants the
best possible compiler to fairly demonstrate the capability of an architecture, yet it may take years for a compiler to mature and adequately
exploit the architecture. So it would seem that fair assessment of a
machine can only be done as a retrospective exercise for an architecture successful enough to warrant continuous compiler development.
Fortunately, compiler technology is advancing and is much more easily
targeted to a new architecture.

The consequence of such an overwhelming influence on the instruction stream is to force comparisons to be very specific and adjustments
estimated to account for these influences. For example, in the earlier
chapter, VAX instruction data were adjusted to reflect what would have
happened had the compiler generated shorter displacements to global
data.

"halve" permits a potentially smaller program representation and an
optimized execution. A floating-point divide is a difficult operation,
but a floating-point halve can be very fast. This illustrates the two
major machine-dependent effects. First, the size of a representation
is more highly encoded. Frequently occurring sequences are replaced
with special instructions and common operands are either implicit in
the instruction or encoded in the operand specifier fields. Frequently
accessed variables are encoded with smaller name specifiers. Second,
machine-dependent effects replace frequently executed sequences with
faster mechanisms. The use of registers reflects both of these effects;
the name of a variable is smaller and the access time is reduced.

The storage mechanism used by a variable affects the instruction
stream. When a variable is allocated to a register, either temporary
or permanent, the number of main memory references and size of the
instruction stream is reduced. The ability of compilers to effectively
use registers has changed greatly over the years. The S/370 compilers
span technology from rudimentary to one of the best available.

Registers are only one example of the partitioning of the variable
name space. Stack architectures store intermediate values in implicit
high-speed-register structures. The variable specifier can be eliminated
from the instruction stream, by producing smaller instructions. Normally, the interior of the stack can be addressed explicitly but the access
time reverts to a speed similar to main memory references. Stack architectures restrict the highest speed storage cells to one or two elements,
so it is very difficult to allocate program variables to stack storage.

Determining the size of the register file involves a great many trade-offs. The size of a program grows if the number of registers is made larger. For the S/370 architecture, if the number of registers were doubled from 16 to 32 the register field size would increase to 5 bits. Ignoring any instruction alignment issues, the dynamic instruction stream size would increase by 10 percent (Fortran Hopt1 averages). If the VAX register set were doubled, the dynamic instruction stream size would increase by only four percent.

Tempering all of these decisions is the potential need to save and restore allocated registers between environment changes. Variables mapped to main memory are most often referenced by adding a base register to a displacement. Short displacement fields distinguish program variables by changing the base registers when environments are changed. In that way the displacement field need only cover the variables in any single environment and not span all of the program variables. Registers are also mapped to some subset of the program variables, but a switch to a new environment requires that some of the registers be reallocated. To illustrate, consider the program counter for the VAX as a register allocated to reference labels. Within a procedure, it is used to branch to nearby destinations with small, easily decoded instructions. At procedure call, the program counter is copied to a main memory cell and copied back when the procedure returns.

The optimization of constants that appear in the high-level-language representation or are generated by the compiler is a function of the host architecture. Many mechanisms exist to reduce the space–time cost of referencing a constant. The distribution of constants is non-uniform, as seen in the last chapter. Some use of the often-referenced constants may be the result of inadequate optimization.

Peep-hole optimization covers several methods of simplifying small sequences of instructions. For example, instructions may produce alternate methods to reference variables. After calculating an expression and storing the result (on a register architecture) a duplicate of that variable exists in the register file. Under certain conditions a subsequent reference to that variable may use the copy in the register file. A stack architecture cannot take advantage of such a situation. However, it would be possible if a read reference directly followed a stack store for the same variable to first duplicate the top of stack and then store the variable (thus saving the read reference).

Side effects of program execution can be capitalized on. The condition codes may contain the correct condition and avoid a redundant test or comparison. A divide instruction may generate a reminder needed later in execution. A string search may generate both an offset, direct address, and condition in one instruction. In each case the optimization could not be performed on an earlier representation of the program (e.g., code tree, quads) since the side effects are not known until the machine code is generated.

Address calculations can be optimized on many architectures. The VAX allows many different mechanisms to reference program variables. Constants can be considered a special case. The effective address computation performed by an architecture serves to partition fixed-point arithmetic. In a high-speed implementation of an architecture, greater concurrency is possible since fewer dependencies occur. Consider an array index operation. A S/370 instruction sequence needs to scale the index in one instruction and then add the base of the array in an address calculation in the second instruction. It is necessary for the execution of the scaling instruction to complete before the address computation of the next instruction can begin. A VAX instruction can combine the scaling operation into a single address calculation. While both sequences do the same work, the VAX may (potentially) perform other simultaneous computations. While the current VAX implementations cannot take advantage of this concurrency, it is possible to implement architectures that exploit optimized address calculations.

The instruction stream changes dramatically when machine-dependent optimizations are performed. The bulk of these differences occur in the variable reference behavior. Traditional load/store architectures can greatly reduce the memory traffic if register allocation is properly performed. The size of a representation can be decreased by short variable name specifiers. In some cases the variable is implicit in the instruction (ex., **clear**); in others the value is explicit (ex., immediates). Certain control functions (ex., **odd**) can be provided by the architecture to reduce conditional branching. As shown in the previous chapter and supported by other studies, the frequency of the optimization is very low.

4.6:   Case Study

The instruction stream produced by executing the test set of programs by the four architectures cannot be directly used for comparisons. The earlier sections of this chapter qualified the term *compiler effects*. The process of compilation introduces differences in the instruction streams due to the techniques and optimizations used to generate machine code. In this section, the results discussed in the previous chapter are examined again to estimate the compiler effects and make a few more specific architectural comparisons. Further, the changes in the instruction stream due to improving compiler technologies are highlighted.

Machine Dependent Effects

These effects are the direct consequences of architecture and represent the information that leads to direct architectural comparison. "How many registers are needed? How are condition codes used? What are the operands to conditional branches? How effective are index registers?" These are some of the questions that measurements of machine dependent effects can answer.

Unfortunately, the other compiler effects must first be reconciled before answers are available. For example, the HP-PA design team struggled with the architectural feature of a unit indexed (scale by the size of the data operand) addressing mode. No compiler, at the time, fully optimized indexed operations into the equivalent induction variables. The designers could not adjust their measurements of index register use because the machine independent effect of induction variable creation could not be estimated. In the end, the HP-PA designers included indexed addressing. No current data support or refute that choice.

It is important to understand the types of optimization utilized by the different compilers. Consider the following procedure used by the Sort program to verify that an array is correctly sorted:

```
SUBROUTINE CHECK
COMMON N,M,FAIL,X,COUNT,AKEY(100) ...
INTEGER N,M,FAIL,X,COUNT,AKEY,I,NM1
NM1 = N-1
DO 10 I = 1,NM1
    IF( AKEY(I) .GT. AKEY(I+1) ) FAIL = 1
10 CONTINUE
RETURN
END
```

This procedure was chosen to illustrate the many different optimizations that are possible.

The S/370 code produced by the Fortran G and Hopt0 compilers is listed in Table 4.11. The notation is similar to the S/370 assembly language. FP is register 13 and points to the local activation record. The Hopt0 compiler produced the simplest code. Registers are used to hold intermediate values and register names are reused. The addition of the constant 1 in the expression AKEY(I+1) is optimized into the displacement field of an address calculation. The G and H compilers use label pointers to branch conditionally. A register is first loaded with the address of the label and conditionally used as the branch target.

Table 4.11: S/370 Fortran G and Hopt0 compiler output.

		Fortran G				Fortran Hopt0	
Lab	Opcode	Operand	Comment	Lab	Opcode	Operand	Comment
	Load	R10,72(FP)	Common		Load	R7,104(FP)	Common
	Load	R0,0(R10)	N		Load	R0,0(R7)	N
	Sub	R0,180(FP)	1		Sub	R0,80(FP)	1
	Str	R0,112(FP)	NM1		Str	R0,88(FP)	NM1
	Load	R7,160(FP)	adr AKEY[1]		Load	R0,80(FP)	1
	Load	R0,180(FP)	1		Str	R0,84(FP)	I
LOOP:				LOOP:			
	Str	R0,108(FP)	I		Load	R6,84(FP)	I
					SLL	R6,2	I*4
					Load	R7,104(FP)	Common
	Load	R0,20(R7)	AKEY[I]		Load	R0,16(R6,R7)	AKEY[I]
					Str	R0,108(FP)	temp
					Load	R6,84(FP)	I
					SLL	R6,2	I*4
					Load	R0,108(FP)	temp
	Comp	R0,24(R7)	AKEY[I+1]		Comp	R0,20(R6,R7)	AKEY[I+1]
	Load	R14,104(FP)	NOTIF		Load	R5,128(FP)	NOTIF
	BrCond	LE,R14	BrCond			LE,R5	
THEN:				THEN:			
	Load	R0,180(FP)	1		Load	R0,80(FP)	1
	Load	R11,72(FP)	Common		Load	R7,104(FP)	Common
	Str	R0,8(R11)	FAIL		Str	R0,8(R7)	FAIL
NOTIF:				NOTIF:			
	Add	R7,184(FP)	4		Load	R0,84(R13)	I
	Load	R0,108(FP)	I		Add	R0,80(R13)	1
	Load	R1,100(FP)	LOOP		Str	R0,84(FP)	I
	LdAdr	R2,1(0,0)	1		Comp	R0,88(FP)	NM1
	Load	R3,112(FP)	NM1		Load	R5,120(FP)	LOOP
	BXLE	R0,R2,0(R1)	Add, Compare, and Branch Less or Equal		BrCond	LE,R5	

CHAPTER 4. COMPILER EFFECTS

Compiler Speed

A common criticism of optimization is the increased compilation time. The compilation time for each of our test programs was averaged to determine the "cost" of the S/370 Fortran optimization. Relative to the Hopt1 compilation time, a Hopt0 compilation is 20 percent faster, a Hopt2 compilation is 60 percent slower, and a Hopt3 compilation is 72 percent slower. As shown later in this chapter, the code produced by the Hopt3 compiler (and therefore the compiler itself) is, on the average, 43 percent faster than Hopt1. Therefore, when optimized at Hopt3 levels the IBM Fortran compiler can produce Hopt3 level code slightly faster than it can, when optimized at Hopt1 levels, produce Hopt1 code. The comparison of Hopt0 to Hopt3 levels is even more pronounced, with a 22% advantage. The actual values for the compiler [57] show an improvement even better than these estimates. These data support the positive effect on net execution time by advanced optimization techniques.

Table 4.12: S/370 Fortran G and Hopt0 summaries for CHECK routine.

	G		Hopt0	
Instructions	6+11n	(1095)	6+17n	(1689)
Memory Reads	5+7n	(698)	4+11n	(1093)
Memory Writes	1+n	(100)	2+2n	(200)

The G compiler performed a form of induction variable elimination. The calculation of array address AKEY[I] is converted to a single pointer that is incremented by the element size each time through the loop. This CCV is also allocated to a register. The loop control sequence for the G and Hopt0 compilers does about the same amount of work. The G compiler uses a BXLE instruction and the Hopt0 compiler explicitly does add, compare, and branch on less or equal. Since the loop's control variables were not allocated to registers, the BXLE instruction does not save memory references or instructions. Table 4.12 summarizes the instruction counts and memory references as a function of the number of times through the loop (n). The logical IF statement is always false. The value in parentheses shows the results for $n = 99$. The array calculation optimization in the G compiler reduces the instruction count by 35 percent.

Now consider the code produced by the other levels of optimizations. In this example, the Hopt2 and Hopt3 compilers produce the same instruction sequence. Table 4.13 lists the instructions generated by the

S/370 Fortran Hopt1 and 2 compilers. The Hopt1 compiler does register allocation for the array base and control variables, but is still unable to avoid the duplicate index calculation $I * 4$. The branch instructions now use a base register to avoid referencing a label. After loop termination, the Hopt1 compiler uses a conservative approach that updates all the variables in main memory. The variable N is invariant in this case and did not need to be rewritten. The Hopt2 compiler correctly stored the only variable that could be changed and produce a side effect.

The loops were optimized to eliminate all memory references except those to the array elements. The control variable update uses registers and careful register assignment allows the Hopt2 compiler to use the BXLE instruction, thus saving two instructions per iteration. None of the compilers attempted to unroll the loop and recognize that the $I + 1^{st}$ element of one iteration is the Ith element of the next iteration. This optimization reduced memory references to one access per iteration. Table 4.14 summarizes the instruction counts and memory reference behavior. The instruction counts are dramatically reduced by the induction variable elimination of the Hopt2 compiler, but the memory traffic is largely unaffected. The Hopt2 compiler is a four times improvement over the unoptimized output in the number of instructions and a five-fold improvement in the number of memory references. The S/370 Pascal/VS compiler does not allocate registers but does keep track of intermediate results in basic blocks. It also uses the more efficient base register branch instructions. This example exaggerates the improvement made with optimizing compilers. The data presented later in this section serve to better gauge the magnitude of improvement that can be expected for a scientific work load.

4.6.1: Instruction Stream

As discussed before, comparing an architectural measure such as "instructions executed" is complicated, since not only architectural differences but also compiler differences affect the value. To quantify the compiler effects, the next sections examine the execution of the different compilers on a single architecture so that all of the differences in the various measures can only be the result of compiler effects.

Static Size

Compiler optimizations that move code out of loops do not change the size of a program. When alternate names are generated for loop invariants, the program size can increase. Register allocation reduces the program size because smaller variable specifiers are used, but the

Table 4.13: S/370 Fortran Hopt1 and Hopt2 compiler output.

Fortran Hopt1				Fortran Hopt2 and Hopt3			
Lab	Opcode	Operand	Comment	Lab	Opcode	Operand	Comment
	Load	R9,112(FP)	Common		Load	R8,112(FP)	Common
	Load	R11,92(FP)	I		Load	R10,116(FP)	4
	Load	R10,80(FP)	1		Load	R7,80(FP)	1
	Load	R8,96(FP)	NM1		Load	R11,0(R8)	N
	Load	R7,8(R9)	FAIL		Sub	R11,R7	form NM1
	Load	R6,0(R9)	N		SLL	R11,2	
	Load	R11,R10	1		Load	R6,8(0,R8)	FAIL
	Load	R8,R6	N		Load	R9,R10	4
	Sub	R8,R10	form NM1				
LOOP:				LOOP:			
	Load	R3,R11	I				
	SLL	R3,2					
	Load	R2,16(R3,R9)	AKEY[I]		Load	R2,16(9,8)	AKEY[I]
	Load	R3,R11	I				
	SLL	R3,2					
	Comp	R2,20(R3,R9)	AKEY[I+1]		Comp	R2,20(R9,R8)	AKEY[I+1]
	BrCond	LE,174(FP)	NOTIF		BrCond	LE,170(FP)	NOTIF
THEN:				THEN:			
	Load	R7,R10	1		Load	R6,R7	1
NOTIF:				NOTIF:			
	Add	R11,R10	inc I				
	Comp	R11,R8	NM1				
	BrCond	LE,148(FP)	LOOP		BXLE	R9,R10,156(FP)	Add, Compare, and Branch Less or Equal
	Str	R6,0(R9)	N		Str	R6,8(R8)	FAIL
	Str	R7,8(R9)	FAIL				
	Str	R8,96(FP)	NM1				
	Str	R11,92(FP)	I				

Table 4.14: S/370 Fortran Hopt1, 2, and 3 summaries for CHECK routine.

	Hopt1	Hopt2 and 3
Instructions	13+10n (1003)	9+4n (405)
Memory Reads	6+2n (204)	5+2n (203)
Memory Writes	4 (4)	1 (1)

Table 4.15: S/370 relative program size (per CI operation).

		FFT	Mort	Norm	Sort	Average
CI		1	1	1	1	1
	G	10.3	5.1	6.7	9.3	7.8
S/370	Hopt0	12.1	5.2	8.6	9.4	8.8
Fortran	Hopt1	8.7	3.8	5.6	6.9	6.2
	Hopt2	7.4	3.6	4.8	6.3	5.5
	Hopt3	7.4	3.7	4.7	6.3	5.5
S/370 Pascal/VS		7.8	4.7	5.4	6.8	6.2

savings depend on the frequency of that allocated variable. Table 4.15 summarizes the program sizes for the different compilers relative to the CI measure.

The percentage difference between the largest and smallest representations is 38 percent. The Hopt0 appears to be an exceptionally poor representation. The code produced by the Hopt0 compilers is very similar to the P-code machine. S/370 registers replace the stack and no effort is made to use intermediate results or to allocate variables to registers. The S/370 Hopt0 references main memory the same as the P-code machine, and must include register specifiers where the P-code machine could imply a stack operand. If compared to the P-code static size of 10.12 (bytes per CI byte), the S/370 representation is more compact. But if the adjusted static size recoded zero operand instructions into one byte, then the P-code static size of 8.2 is slightly smaller. This indicates that the naive compiler's representation is dominated by the memory operand specifiers and the architectural differences not related to memory specifiers contribute little to the size of a program.

The highly optimized Hopt2 and Hopt3 representation only slightly improves the Hopt1 results (12 percent). The largest improvement occurred in the FFT and Norm programs, 15 and 16 percent respectively. These programs have the highest frequency of loop structures and array references for which optimizations are most space effective.

The discussion of compiler effects examined the kinds of changes that optimization makes on the instruction stream. In this section the magnitude of these effects is examined. Returning to the most fundamental measure of instruction set performance, consider the relative instruction counts shown in Table 4.16. The Hopt0 result is 2.8 times the average Hopt3 compiler's values. In fact, the Hopt3 compiler produces code that executes 11 percent fewer instructions than the VAX/UNIX Fortran compilers (average relative value = 1.99). The greatest improvement occurred for the FFT and Norm programs. The discussion on static size showed the same grouping. If only FFT and Norm are included, the improvement by the Hopt3 compiler is 3.7 times over the Hopt0 compiler. When the Mort and Sort programs are grouped, only a 1.8 times improvement exists. The FFT and Norm programs contain language constructs and an execution profile that allowed greater gains through optimization. Arrays are referenced more often, and by examining the source program it is evident that a large portion of these references occur in loop constructs.

Table 4.17 summarizes the Gibson classifications for the composite work load. The values in parentheses show the percentages within a given column. The greatest changes occur to the *move* class. The Hopt3 compiler reduced the number of moves by a factor of 3.8 times. Even the Hopt1 compiler was able to reduce the number of moves to less than half of the value for the Hopt0 compiler. Other computational classes also decrease with increasing optimization. The *fix add/sub* class is reduced by a smaller fraction, but the array indexing class *shift* was reduced by a factor of over four. The more specialized classes, *floating point* and *fix divide*, are relatively unaffected by the optimizations. The *fix multiply* class improvement can be traced to a two dimensional array calculation optimization in the Norm program.

The elimination of array index calculations by the optimizing compiler is most dramatic, but the reduction in the *move* class makes the greatest absolute difference in the results. Table 4.18 lists the different instructions that comprise the *move* class. The most frequent move instructions are the memory-to-register load instructions—LOAD(RX), LOAD(RXFLT. SHORT), and LOAD(RXFLT. LONG). With lesser optimization (G and Hopt0), over 65 percent of the move instructions were simple memory-to-register loads. The better compilers reduced this fraction to around 45 percent of the moves.

The store instructions are least affected. Register allocation, common subexpression elimination and code hoisting optimizations reduce the number of computations and hence the number of times a memory

Table 4.16: S/370 executed instructions (per CI operation).

CI		FFT	Mort	Norm	Sort	Average
CI		1	1	1	1	1
S/370 Fortran	G	4.76	3.47	4.50	3.01	3.93
	Hopt0	7.19	3.23	6.03	3.28	4.93
	Hopt1	4.27	2.21	3.79	2.11	3.10
	Hopt2	2.34	1.83	1.40	1.73	1.83
	Hopt3	2.30	1.82	1.26	1.73	1.78
S/370 Pascal/VS		3.57	2.97	3.04	2.66	3.06

Table 4.17: S/370 Gibson classification (per thousand CI operations).

| Gibson Class | G | Fortran | | | | Pascal/VS |
		Hopt0	Hopt1	Hopt2	Hopt3	
Move	2,288 (58)	3,311 (67)	1,489 (48)	861 (47)	858 (48)	1,477 (48)
Fix Add/Sub	505 (13)	267 (5.6)	276 (8.9)	183 (10)	140 (7.8)	548 (18)
Branch	314 (8.0)	263 (5.3)	263 (8.5)	264 (14)	264 (15)	253 (8.3)
Shift	301 (7.7)	524 (11)	524 (17)	124 (6.8)	123 (6.9)	256 (8.4)
Compare	164 (4.2)	198 (4.0)	198 (6.4)	129 (7.0)	128 (7.2)	198 (6.5)
Float Add/Sub	145 (3.7)	147 (3.0)	134 (4.3)	130 (7.1)	130 (7.3)	154 (5.0)
Float Multiply	105 (2.7)	105 (2.1)	105 (3.4)	104 (5.7)	104 (5.8)	105 (3.4)
Fix Multiply	85 (2.2)	76 (1.5)	76 (2.5)	7.9 (.4)	7.8 (.4)	45 (1.5)
Fix Divide	10 (.2)	10 (.2)	10 (.3)	10 (.5)	10 (.5)	–
Float Divide	7 (.2)	7 (.1)	7 (.2)	7 (.4)	7 (.4)	7 (.2)
Boolean	6 (.1)	–	–	–	–	–
Logical	–	11 (.2)	11 (.3)	11 (.3)	6 (.3)	6 (.3)

Table 4.18: S/370 Move class distribution (per million CI operations).

	G	Fortran				Pascal/VS
		Hopt0	Hopt1	Hopt2	Hopt3	
LOAD(RX)	1,304,099	1,697,233	329,693	237,992	235,978	664,928
STORE(RX)	311,922	459,183	123,372	124,694	124,286	215,227
LOAD(RXFLT. SHORT)	157,548	352,865	238,723	109,093	109,093	0
STORE(RXFLT. SHORT)	129,488	355,482	116,418	96,457	96,457	0
LOAD(RR)	117,095	134,078	477,358	125,917	124,963	261,634
LOAD ADDRESS(RX)	83,148	5,907	5,907	5,907	5,907	9,452
LOAD(RXFLT. LONG)	71,118	135,011	91,306	46,753	46,753	129,445
STORE(RXFLT. LONG)	52,311	132,309	53,820	51,075	51,075	103,523
MOVE CHARACTER(SS)	18,651	0	0	0	0	54,817
LOAD AND TEST(RR)	16,581	23,385	23,385	23,385	23,385	24,383
LOAD(RRFLT. SHORT)	10,594	0	12,475	4,990	4,990	0
STORE MULTIPLE(RS)	6,286	3,258	3,258	3,027	3,259	2,976
LOAD MULTIPLE(RS)	6,046	9,138	9,138	9,138	9,138	3,063
MOVE IMMEDIATE(SI)	3,166	3,182	3,182	3,182	3,182	292
LOAD(RRFLT. LONG)	0	0	528	19,769	19,769	7,383
LOAD AND TEST (RRFLT.)	41	64	64	64	64	95
Total	2,288,094	3,311,095	1,488,627	861,443	858,299	1,477,218

location is read, but the data indicate that the frequency of store operations is less affected. The store frequency for the G, H, and Pascal/VS compilers (per CI operation) is .50, .95, .30, .28, .28, and .32, respectively. As seen by the example in an earlier section, the large Hopt0 value reflects the creation of CCV's for intermediate array address calculations. The Hopt1, 2, and 3 compilers eliminate the store of the control variable, but few others are eliminated. The Pascal/VS compiler did not optimize loop control variables, yet the number of stores is similar in value (at worst 14 percent different). More recent efforts in optimization [7] have significantly reduced the number of memory references for machines with a larger number of registers, but the breakdown to determine the frequency of write references is not available in the literature. The frequency of instructions (per CI operation) that store into main memory for the other architectures is quite similar: .34 and .35 for the P-code and VAX (UNIX), respectively. The VAX figure excludes the FFT program because of an unfair (to the VAX) compilation of the COMPLEX data type.

The number of instructions decreased by optimization and also by the type of instruction changed. Since the number of memory-to-register instructions decreased, the relative frequency of register-to-register instructions increased (10 percent to 22 percent). Table 4.19 summarizes the instruction activities for the S/370 compilers. The machine independent optimizations of the S/370 Hopt3 compiler can be used to estimate VAX optimized machine code. Even the machine-dependent optimizations can be used for the VAX estimate since it also has 16 registers. The majority of the improvement by the S/370 compilers came from reduced register-to-memory loads and address computations (shifts). As a best-case estimate (for the VAX), assume all of the remaining memory-to-register load instructions by the S/370 Hopt3 compiler could be eliminated by the VAX memory-to-memory architecture. The comparable VAX figure would become 1.39 (1.78–.391 loads): a 22 percent improvement. Consider the Gibson class for the VAX compared with the S/370 Hopt3. The *branch, shift, compare,* and *floating-ops* classes are similar. The difference in the *fix multiply* value can be traced to the optimization of a two-dimensional array access. This gives a comparable VAX value of 1.31 (per CI operation). The three operand instructions of the VAX reduce the need for a store instruction. Assume all of the store instructions would be unnecessary, then a comparable VAX value of 1.04 would result (a 42 percent reduction). This compares favorably to actual measured VAX data of 1.14 (see Table 3.14 b) that does not include a Mort result.

A lower bound on number of "instruction objects" needed by the VAX can be calculated by using the register references that S/370 made ex-

Table 4.19: S/370 instruction activities (average per CI operation).

| | | Fortran | | | | Pascal/VS |
	G	Hopt0	Hopt1	Hopt2	Hopt3	
Instructions	3.93	4.93	3.10	1.83	1.78	3.06
Bytes Fetched	14.8	18.7	10.4	6.4	6.3	11.4
Instruction Objects	7.4	9.4	5.2	3.2	3.2	5.6

clusive of the load and store instructions. A register reference on S/370 would map a mode/register specifier on VAX. The memory references will also add a displacement field specifier. The lower limit is therefore:

$$1.03(\text{Opcode}) + 2.79(\text{Register Spec.}) - 2 \times .67(\text{Load+Stores}) + 1.0(\text{Disp.}) = 3.49$$

Given a most optimistic development, the VAX architecture executes 42 percent fewer instructions but requires a greater number of instruction objects. The time to interpret the S/370 and VAX instruction streams depends on the implementation of the architecture and the degree of parallelism that is achieved. The data on VAX/VMS execution do not allow the calculation of instruction objects.

While the number of move and fixed-point arithmetic instructions is reduced by optimization, certain of the Gibson classes remain constant. Earlier in this chapter, invariant effects were described and two significant instruction classes were included. Floating-point operations are again shown to be largely invariant to optimization by the Gibson classification. Since the absolute occurrence is constant, the relative frequency will increase with better optimization. Table 4.20 summarizes the relative frequency of floating-point operations for all of the compilers and machines used in this study. The P-code compiler has the lowest frequency of floating-point operators, since it has the greatest instruction count. The highest frequency of floating-point operations is produced by the compiler with the most sophisticated optimization—S/370 Hopt3.

This distribution is not uniform; the Mort and Sort programs contained no floating point, but programs that contain floating point can have very high relative frequencies. The Norm program CI floating-point operation frequency is 45 percent. The frequency ranged from 7.92 percent (P-code) to 39.4 percent (S/370 Hopt3). Machine designers must adjust the expected floating-point frequencies when work loads warrant it.

Invariant compiler effects fix the absolute occurrence of control operations. The *branch* and *compare* classes reflect this effect. The use

Table 4.20: Floating-point frequency as percent of executed instructions (average).

		Add/Sub	Multiply	Divide	Totals
CI		8.1	6.7	.7	15.5
	G	3.7	2.7	.2	6.6
S/370	Hopt0	3.0	2.1	.1	5.2
Fortran	Hopt1	4.3	3.4	.2	7.9
	Hopt2	7.1	5.7	.4	13.2
	Hopt3	7.3	5.8	.4	13.5
S/370	Pascal/VS	5.0	3.4	.2	8.6
P-Code	Pascal	2.6	1.9	.1	4.7
VAX/UNIX	Fortran	6.1	5.3	.3	11.7

of the BXLE instruction reduces the S/370 Hopt2 and 3 results for the *compare* class by 70 counts per thousand CI operations. The relative frequency of branch instructions for all of the architectures varies from a low of 4.6 percent (P-code) to a high of 15 percent (S/370 Hopt3). Increased optimization in this case triples the frequency of branch instructions.

Studies that have used more advanced compilers for the VAX [72] show a higher fraction of branch instructions. In that study, 31 percent of the VAX instructions were potential branches. The work load was an average of several compilers with a range of sophistication. For comparison, an S/370 study on the execution of the H compiler [59], itself optimized at opt level 2, reported an S/370 branch frequency of 21.6 percent.

The composition of instruction types in the instruction stream changes with optimization. The absolute frequency of RR (register-to-register) instructions is largely the same for all of the S/370 compilers except the Hopt1 compiler. For the others, roughly 400 RR instructions are executed per 1000 CI operations. Because the absolute occurrence is constant, the relative frequency increased from 9.9 percent to 24 percent of the instructions. The Hopt1 compiler is double the expected value because of a machine-independent effect that copies registers before a shift and index operation. If those register-to-register copies are eliminated, we get a consistent figure of 21 percent.

The register specifier fields are also affected by increasing optimization. The relative frequency of register references is shown in Table 4.21. The difference results from the use of the index register. The S/370 Hopt3 compiler used 46 percent of the potential index register fields, while the S/370 G compiler used only 14 percent of the available fields. The absolute number of index fields utilized does not change;

CHAPTER 4. COMPILER EFFECTS

Table 4.21: S/370 register references (averages per executed instruction).

S/370		Register References		Total
		Read	Write	
Fortran	G	1.51	.77	2.28
	Hopt0	1.47	.71	2.18
	Hopt1	1.55	.75	2.30
	Hopt2	1.83	.67	2.50
	Hopt3	1.83	.66	2.49
Pascal/VS		1.58	.73	2.30

Table 4.22: S/370 register references used as an address.

S/370		Fraction of total register references as an address*
Fortran	G	.64
	Hopt0	.69
	Hopt1	.56
	Hopt2	.55
	Hopt3	.57

*Includes shift instructions.

rather the reduction in the total number of instructions increases the relative frequency. The use of registers as addresses was shown in the last chapter to represent a very large fraction of register read references. The fraction of total register references used as an address for the S/370 compilers is shown in Table 4.22.

There are two mechanisms that work to keep the percentage somewhat constant. Higher optimization levels allocate data objects in registers and reduce the base-displacement references to those objects. This reduces the register address references, but the increased use of induction variables and the more effective use of index registers decreases the number of data references and address arithmetic (which is not distinguishable from, and consequently counts as, data references).

The most common use of registers as addresses occurs in base plus index plus displacement effective address calculations. In the last chapter, the distribution of base and index registers was highly skewed to a few registers. Table 4.23 shows the base register distribution for the S/370 compilers. Increased optimization has little effect on the skew in the distribution. The four most referenced base registers for each compiler account for over 80 percent of all references. R13 is used by each compiler as a local frame pointer. These data again support the

Table 4.23: S/370 base register distribution (average per thousand CI operations).

S/370	Fortran					Pascal/VS
	G	Hopt0	Hopt1	Hopt2	Hopt3	
Excluded	83	4.5	4.5	4.5	4.5	2.6
R1	23	3.9	3.9	3.9	3.9	11
R2	3.0	1.1	1.1	1.1	1.3	483
R3	–	2.7	2.7	5.5	5.3	283
R4	3.2	3.1	3.1	5.4	4.2	161
R5	.3	.2	.2	75	45	26
R6	42	–	7.6	138	57	10
R7	70	619	11	202	204	25
R8	–	2.9	145	64	152	6.6
R9	–	2.9	106	9.3	12	40
R10	200	5.8	115	15	36	213
R11	189	6.3	251	97	97	39
R12	135	17	36	14	14	30
R13	2,287	3,227	824	542	528	856
R14	21	.3	–	–	.3	–
R15	9.6	3.4	39	4.3	4.0	–

use of specific functions in dedicated registers to reduce the need for wider base register specifiers.

The index register distribution is changed by the optimization of the S/370 compiler. The S/370 Fortran G, Hopt0, and Pascal/VS compilers use only two to four index registers for nearly all of the references. The Hopt2 and Hopt3 compilers distributed these same references over nine index registers. Induction variable optimization often allows the direct use of a CCV in an address computation. The simpler mechanism in the Hopt1 compiler required that a copy of an index first be made and then an address computation performed. This compiler requires far fewer index registers.

The base and index register specifiers account for between 12.9 and 14.5 percent of the instruction stream. Reducing the number of base registers would not significantly change the size of the instruction stream, but the tradeoffs for some particular instruction could justify trimming the base register field size.

The displacement field distribution is mostly unaffected by optimization. The $\log_2$ of the values is uniformly distributed throughout the 12-bit displacement field. The single exception is the value zero. If the displacement field is not needed, it is still necessary to include it. The PDP-11 and VAX architectures allow a separate address mode if no dis-

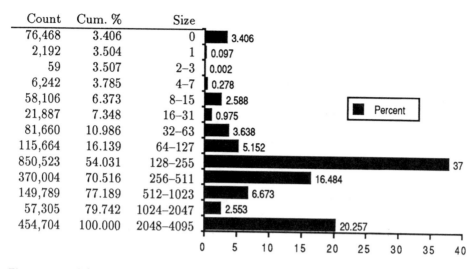

Count	Cum. %	Size
76,468	3.406	0
2,192	3.504	1
59	3.507	2–3
6,242	3.785	4–7
58,106	6.373	8–15
21,887	7.348	16–31
81,660	10.986	32–63
115,664	16.139	64–127
850,523	54.031	128–255
370,004	70.516	256–511
149,789	77.189	512–1023
57,305	79.742	1024–2047
454,704	100.000	2048–4095

Figure 4.1: S/370 displacement field distribution (average per million CI operations).

placement is needed (e.g., register deferred). The S/370 Hopt1 compiler uses a zero displacement field in 20 percent of the memory to register (RX) instructions. The VAX compiler uses register deferred mode in 19.82 of the memory references. The displacement field accounts for between 30.2 and 35.6 percent of the S/370 instruction stream. A re-encoding to eliminate zero displacement fields could reduce the dynamic instruction stream by 7 percent.

The displacement field distribution for the Pascal/VS execution illustrates the changes to an instruction stream due to a compiler effect. Figure 4.1 shows the memory-to-register D-field distribution. Pascal/VS local variables and parameters are stored in a dynamic storage area referenced by base register 13. The first 144 bytes of this region are reserved by the run-time system for register save areas and several internal linkage pointers. Next, the parameter list and local variables are stored. The D-field distribution is biased to the values 128–511. Of the 2.2 million counts, 846,154 (38 percent) use register 13. The organization of the dynamic save area produced larger displacement values than necessary. If reorganized, a very different distribution would have resulted. The compiler has a great deal of latitude in determining the displacement values needed in activation record (e.g., dynamic variable) addressing. The symmetric byte displacement of the VAX is never used by the Fortran compiler. The lack of negative offsets in the S/370 does not create a problem for the Pascal/VS compiler. Pointers are created such that only positive displacements are needed. Compile time optimizations can be used by the instruction set designer to better use the fields of an instruction.

Table 4.24: Memory reads/writes (totals in thousands).

		Memory reads				Memory writes			
		FFT	Mort	Norm	Sort	FFT	Mort	Norm	Sort
CI		105	4,696	1,236	1,244	23	567	208	247
	G	147	6,270	1,773	1,301	46	618	365	258
S/370	Hopt0	221	5,425	2,195	1,348	95	964	730	295
Fortran	Hopt1	72	2,926	638	369	29	586	178	97
	Hopt2	53	2,219	403	292	24	614	157	108
	Hopt3	51	2,208	397	292	24	614	156	108
S/370 Pascal/VS		110	3,760	1,222	987	27	589	274	247

4.6.2: Memory Referencing

Compiler optimization attempts to reduce the resource demands of a
program on an architecture. In the last section, the instruction stream
was analyzed. In this section, the storage mechanisms of an architecture are examined. The compiler attempts to map a source program to
a host architecture in the most efficient manner. The variables in a program are usually mapped to a homogeneous storage mechanism such as
main memory. Registers, on the other hand, are an architectural feature that are available to the compiler to allow faster access to a small
and possibly changing subset of the program's variables. In some architectures, registers are a necessary staging area for computations. For
example, S/370 stores only the result of fixed-point or floating-point
operations into a register. Allocating a program variable or intermediate computation to a register can significantly reduce the number of
references to main memory. In the CHECK subroutine example, the
number of memory references is reduced by a factor of five. A further
optimization not used by the S/370 H compilers could have reduced it
by an order of magnitude. Table 4.24 summarizes the memory reads
for the S/370 execution. The Hopt3 compiler, in some cases, is over
four times better than the Hopt0 compiler. The Pascal/VS compiler
executes nearly the same number of instructions as the Hopt1 compiler
but references 70 percent more objects in main memory. The memory write statistics for the S/370 compilers show again that the Hopt3
compiler successfully reduces memory write traffic, but the reduction
is not as large as in the read case.

Address Generation

The address of an S/370 memory object is computed in several different ways. Local variables and other simple variables use the current
activation record pointer (e.g., R13) and add a displacement. Register

Table 4.25: Local memory reference fraction (average per memory reference).

S/370		Fraction of local references
Fortran	G	.73
	Hopt0	.81
	Hopt1	.44
	Hopt2	.36
	Hopt3	.35
Pascal/VS		.65

allocation reduces the number of simple memory references by substituting a register reference. The S/370 compilers use register names in a predictable way. Table 4.25 indicates the fraction of local references per memory reference as indicated by the use of the current frame pointer (R13 for Fortran G and H, R13, R2, R10 for Pascal/VS). The register references for branch address calculations are excluded. The CI measures indicate that all but 26 percent of the references should be simple variables.

The decrease in local referencing is complemented by an increase in the number of indexed address calculations for array addressing. The absolute occurrence of index operations (e.g., base + index + displacement) did not change due to optimization. Therefore the relative frequency increased from a low of 14 percent to a high of 46 percent. This greatly changes the address computations seen by an S/370 machine. Simpler compilers produce code that would not justify a three-input adder, but the code produced by the Hopt3 would often use such hardware.

The distribution of displacement field values when the index register is included cannot be determined from the data, but the frequency of a zero D-field did increase from 11.3 percent and 8 percent for Fortran G and Hopt0 to 25 percent for Hopt2 and 3. The Hopt1 compiler generated 20 percent zero D-fields. A check of the compiler listings indicates that the array indexing calculations often specify a zero D-field. If all the zero D-fields are assumed to occur when an index register is specified, then 21 percent of the memory references still require the addition of three operands.

The number of operands used to calculate an effective address changes from compiler effects. The simpler compilers reference operands by using base-displacement addressing, while the more advanced compilers often use base-index-displacement addressing. The increased relative frequency of array address calculations requires the instruction set designer to consider the compiler optimizations in implementation decisions.

Table 4.26: Memory reads by data type (average per CI operation).

S/370		Integer	Real	Other	Total
Fortran	G	2.04	.42	.02	2.48
	Hopt0	2.20	.73	.02	2.95
	Hopt1	.57	.42	.02	1.01
	Hopt2	.39	.32	.02	.73
	Hopt3	.38	.32	.02	.72
Pascal/VS		1.35	.37	.02	1.74

Table 4.27: VAX floating-point read operand specifier fraction (for Norm).

Mode/Register Specifier	Fraction of Floating Operands
Indirect Argument Pointer plus Displacement	.43
Program Counter plus Displacement	.35
Frame Pointer plus Displacement	.13
General Register plus Displacement	.10

Memory Operands

Earlier, compiler optimizations were shown to significantly reduce the number of memory reads and writes. In this section, the reference behavior is broken down to estimate the improvements made by the different compiler effects. Table 4.26 shows the number of read references per CI operation by each of the S/370 compilers. The number of real data objects read is largely the same except for the Hopt0 compiler which saves and restores each intermediate floating-point calculation. The P-code machine's value of .34 floating-point reads per CI operation indicates a machine that does not need to overflow expression evaluation into main memory. The improvement by the Hopt2 and Hopt3 compilers is quite small. From the discussion of compiler invariant effects, we expect floating-point operations to remain constant, but for this work load floating-point memory reads are also generally invariant with compiler optimization. This supports the premise that few common subexpressions exist and there are few candidates among floating-point operands for register allocation. While the distribution of floating-point references by the categories (simple and array) is not directly available, the VAX data provide a good estimate. Table 4.27 shows the mode/register specifiers for the floating-point operands from the Norm program. The 12.8 percent for frame pointer references represents simple accesses.

The 9.6 percent for general register accesses are most likely computed names (e.g., array accesses). Of all the references, 42 percent use the additional operand specifier *index*. Thus, at least 42 percent of all floating-point references could never be optimized. The Hopt2 and 3 compiler performed code hoisting and loop invariant optimizations, but little gain resulted.

The largest reduction of memory references occurs for integer variables. The Hopt1 compiler allocates registers for DO loops and cuts the number of references by 74 percent over the Hopt0 compiler; this gain can be attributed to registers. The FFT and Norm programs experience the largest reduction (7.0 and 8.2 times), since more loop structures are executed. The memory reference frequency for the Mort program is reduced by a factor of only 1.9 by the Hopt1 compiler. There are almost no DO loops, as most of the control flow is implemented using if–goto constructs.

Table 4.28 summarizes the number of memory write references per CI operation for the S/370 compilers. Again, the optimizations do not apply equally to each data type. The floating-point write references are generally the same, except for the Hopt0 anomaly. The superior performance of the Pascal/VS compiler can be traced to a language effect where the move of a complex data object is performed with a single **move character** instruction. The Fortran compilers generated two loads followed by two stores. The P-code compiler generated a move operation to give a result similar to Pascal/VS.

The number of integer store operations is decreased by the optimizations used by the Hopt1 compiler. The more sophisticated code motion and common subexpression optimizations do not reduce memory references. This gives an increased relative frequency of write operations because of a somewhat constant absolute occurrence. Table 4.29 summarizes the relative frequency of memory references for the S/370 compilers. The lowest relative frequency is a result of the Hopt1 compiler and reflects the register allocation optimizations. The Fortran G, Hopt0, and Pascal/VS compilers produce a much higher frequency of memory references because all variable references use main memory. The better optimizations of the Hopt2 and Hopt3 compilers bring the relative frequency back up from the Hopt1 level.

The composition of memory references changes through optimization. The high-level-language test programs specify that 26 percent of the operands are array elements. An array access by the S/370 Fortran H compilers is signaled by the use of an index register. The frequency of specified index registers rose from 14 percent to 46 percent of the RX type (register-to-memory) instructions. The absolute occurrence of index specifiers remained nearly constant (within 26 percent), while the

Table 4.28: Memory writes by data type (average per CI operation).

S/370		Integer	Real	Other	Total
Fortran	G	.31	.18	.03	.52
	Hopt0	.46	.49	.01	.95
	Hopt1	.12	.17	.01	.30
	Hopt2	.12	.15	.01	.28
	Hopt3	.12	.15	.01	.28
Pascal/VS		.24	.13	.01	.38

Table 4.29: S/370 memory references (average per executed instruction).

S/370		Memory References		Total
		Read	Write	
Fortran	G	.63	.13	.76
	Hopt0	.60	.19	.79
	Hopt1	.32	.10	.42
	Hopt2	.40	.15	.56
	Hopt3	.40	.16	.56
Pascal/VS		.57	.13	.70

frequency of RX instructions dropped by more than a factor of three. This again illustrates that compiler effects do not apply uniformly to the instruction stream, but selectively reduce the frequency of certain measures and therefore increase the relative frequency of the other, unaffected measures.

4.6.3:   Control

In an earlier section conditional branch behavior was shown to remain invariant with compiler effects. Unconditional branching statistics change because of the run-time environment used by the compiler. There are some optimizations of loop constructs that reduce unconditional branches. The duplication of loop exit tests or moving the test represents machine-independent optimizations. The DO loop constructs used in this study do not exhibit this behavior.

Branch Instruction Stream

The number of branches relative to the CI measures does not change with optimization, but because the total number of instructions is reduced an optimized instruction stream contains a greater number of branches. Table 4.30 shows the relative percentage and absolute frequency (in parenthesis per thousand CI operations) of branches for the

Table 4.30: S/370 branch percentage and, in parenthesis, frequency (average per thousand CI operations).

S/370		Unconditional		Conditional				Total	
				Taken		Not Taken			
Fortran	G	1.78	(70)	4.22	(166)	2.01	(79)	8.0	(315)
	Hopt0	.81	(40)	2.94	(145)	1.58	(78)	5.3	(263)
	Hopt1	1.26	(39)	4.69	(145)	2.52	(78)	8.5	(262)
	Hopt2	2.19	(40)	9.21	(168)	3.02	(55)	14.4	(263)
	Hopt3	2.25	(40)	9.45	(168)	3.09	(55)	14.8	(263)
Pascal/VS		.98	(30)	4.74	(145)	2.52	(77)	8.3	(252)

S/370 compilers. For example, the Hopt3 execution has 2.25 percent unconditional and a total of 14.8 percent branches. The Fortran G compiler produces a greater number of branches because it expands in-line a formatted I/O's implied DO loop. Removing this gives results consistent with the other compilers.

The total numbers of encountered and taken branches for all of the machines and some of the compilers are shown in Figure 4.2. The S/370 Fortran G, Hopt0, and Hopt1 compilers are excluded since their values closely match the given S/370 results. The values in this figure represent the percentage of excess branches encountered and taken. For example, the VAX/UNIX Fortran compiler generates 21 percent more encountered branches than indicated by the CI measure for branches encountered. The superior performance of the P-code machine is surprising, since many other measures rate it the least efficient.

The poor values for the other machines can be traced to a few specific causes. First, special built-in functions that map to branching structures on one machine may be implemented directly on another machine. For example, the absolute value of an integer maps to a single instruction on the P-code and S/370 architectures, but requires a test and conditional branch to implement the same function on the VAX/UNIX architecture and compiler.

Second, the compilers use different run-time environments. The S/370 and VAX/UNIX compilers branch to procedure prolog and sometimes epilog routines. The VAX/UNIX compiler expands in-line an implied DO loop for an I/O statement. In each case branches are executed that are not required by the architecture but exist because of software structure. Figure 4.3 shows the excess branch percentages when compiler effects are removed. The number of branches encountered for the S/370 Hopt3 compiler is close to the expected value, but 11 percent excess taken branches occurred. The values for the FFT, Norm, and

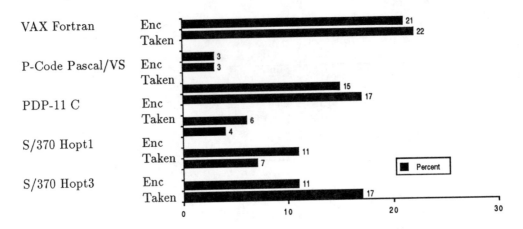

Figure 4.2: Excess branch percentages (average per CI branch).

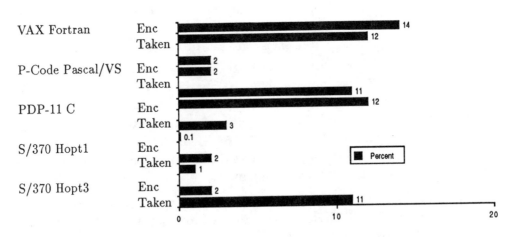

Figure 4.3: Excess branch percentages without compiler effects (average per CI branch).

CHAPTER 4. COMPILER EFFECTS

Sort program are within 1 percent of the expected value. The Mort program, however, shows the number of taken branches to exceed the CI measure by 43 percent. The source of this difference is illustrated by the following statement sequence embedded in a larger loop structure.

```
   ⋮
m := ic;
while marray[m] <> marray[s] do
    begin
    m := m + 2;
    if marray[m+1] <= 0 then goto exitmainloop
    end
   ⋮
```

The variable m was allocated to a register and it is necessary to store the register when the loop terminates. The S/370 Hopt3 compiler generated a conditional branch around two instructions that saved m and unconditionally branched to *exitmainloop*. The CI measure assumed a single conditional branch to *exitmainloop*. The compiler could have first branched to an intermediate location to store m and then branched to *exitmainloop*. The number of conditional branches remains the same, but the number of taken branches increases because the **if** statement outcome is false 95 percent of the time. On the other hand, this optimization produced far fewer instructions and memory references. In this case, the increased number of taken branches is the result of a machine-dependent optimization (register allocation) that is warranted by reductions in other CI measures.

The VAX and PDP-11 results from Figure 4.3 are much higher than expected. Figure 4.4 illustrates the branch mechanisms of the VAX and PDP-11 architectures. The leftmost mechanism in Figure 4.4 illustrates conditional branch to a target that can be reached by an 8-bit displacement. The instruction is two bytes long and the span of the displacement field is 256 and 512 bytes for the VAX and PDP-11 architectures, respectively. If the target is outside the branch span, then the sense of the condition is inverted and an unconditional branch to the true target is inserted. The static instruction stream is made larger and the dynamic instruction stream is changed.

For targets that are within the span of a branch, independent of the conditions value, one conditional branch is encountered. If the condition is true then a branch is taken. For targets outside the branch span, a branch is always taken and two branches are potentially encountered.

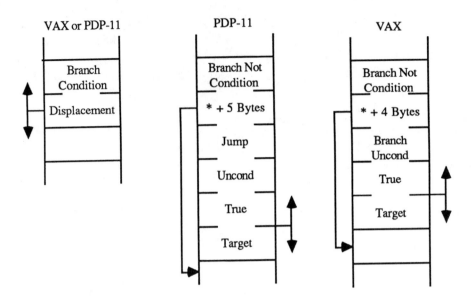

Figure 4.4: VAX and PDP-11 branch mechanisms.

The number of conditional branches remains constant but the total branch measures increase.

The excess branch frequency for the VAX/UNIX and PDP-11 is therefore the result of an architectural difference. The excess frequency of encountered branches ranged from a low of 4 percent (PDP-11 Sort) to a high of 30 percent (PDP-11 FFT). The excess frequency of taken branches ranged from 1 percent (PDP-11 Norm) to 28 percent (PDP-11 Mort). The next subsection examines branch distances in greater detail and is followed by additional discussion of VAX and PDP-11 branch instructions.

The instruction stream of highly optimized programs contains a greater relative frequency of branches and the number of instructions between taken branches (run-length) decreases. Table 4.31 summarizes the run length of the S/370 compilers. The difference between the average and median values highlights the skew to lower run-length values. Run-length medians are expressed as log ranges. This work load contains longer program sequences than would be typical of a system's work load.

The previous chapter discussed the distance to resolve a branch. Optimization does not change the branch resolution distance distribution for branch-on-condition instructions. Nearly all branches depend on the results of the previous instruction. When the S/370 Fortran optimizer uses the BXLE instruction the median resolution distance is more than five instructions. The use of this specialized branch instruction

Table 4.31: S/370 run length (average per executed instruction).

S/370		Run-Length	
		Average	Median
Fortran	G	19.2	8–15
	Hopt0	27.2	16–31
	Hopt1	17.1	8–15
	Hopt2	8.9	4–7
	Hopt3	8.7	4–7
Pascal/VS		17.4	8–15

Table 4.32: VAX/UNIX and PDP-11 span (in bytes and instruction).

VAX/UNIX	PDP-11
256 Bytes	512 Bytes
40 VAX	142 PDP-11
Instructions	Instructions

accounts for over 26 percent of the branch encountered stream (S/370 Hopt2) and allows the computer designer a valuable mechanism to predict branch outcomes.

Branch Distance

Table 4.32 summarizes the VAX and PDP-11 branch span (distance between branch address and its target address) for the conditional branch instructions. The word offsets used by the PDP-11 give twice the span of the byte-oriented VAX instruction stream. The span, in instructions, is estimated by dividing the span in bytes by the average instruction size. Since the VAX executes few instructions, it is likely that a greater coverage is achieved than the 3:1 ratio would indicate. Figure 4.5 shows the distribution of branch distances for the VAX machine. The VAX's 8-bit displacement captures 76 percent of branch targets, whereas the PDP-11 captures 82 percent of its branch targets (from the previous chapter).

The penalty in the instruction stream for a branch beyond the reach of the 8-bit displacement is expensive. The *2–3 Bytes Forward* entry in Figure 4.5 is indicative of this cost. Most likely, all of these branches are the result of complemented conditional branches around a branch to the true target.

4.6. CASE STUDY 143

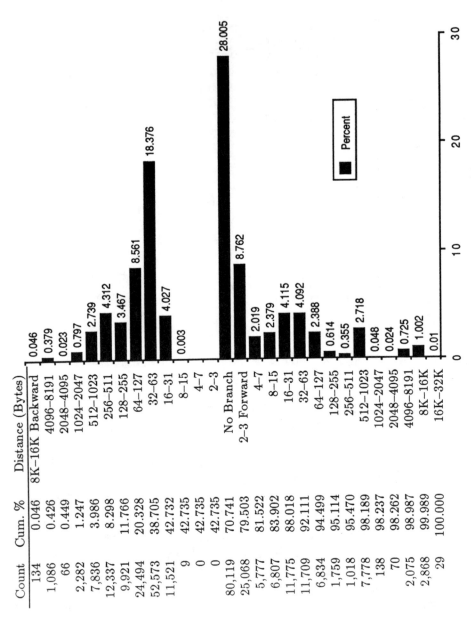

Count	Cum. %	Distance (Bytes)	Percent
134	0.046	8K–16K Backward	0.046
1,086	0.426	4096–8191	0.379
66	0.449	2048–4095	0.023
2,282	1.247	1024–2047	0.797
7,836	3.986	512–1023	2.739
12,337	8.298	256–511	4.312
9,921	11.766	128–255	3.467
24,494	20.328	64–127	8.561
52,573	38.705	32–63	18.376
11,521	42.732	16–31	4.027
9	42.735	8–15	0.003
0	42.735	4–7	
0	42.735	2–3	
80,119	70.741	No Branch	28.005
25,068	79.503	2–3 Forward	8.762
5,777	81.522	4–7	2.019
6,807	83.902	8–15	2.379
11,775	88.018	16–31	4.115
11,709	92.111	32–63	4.092
6,834	94.499	64–127	2.388
1,759	95.114	128–255	0.614
1,018	95.470	256–511	0.355
7,778	98.189	512–1023	2.718
138	98.237	1024–2047	0.048
70	98.262	2048–4095	0.024
2,075	98.987	4096–8191	0.725
2,868	99.989	8K–16K	1.002
29	100.000	16K–32K	0.01

Figure 4.5: VAX/UNIX branch distance distribution (average per thousand CI operations).

In a study of VAX instruction execution [72] the frequency of 1- to 4-byte forward displacements for conditional branches ranged from 3.1 to 16.6 percent. The average for the study was 10.6 percent and the work load was exclusively compiler execution. A study of PDP-11 execution [48] reported the frequency of 8-bit displacements between two and three words forward as 12.8 percent.

In this study, the frequency of 8-bit displacements between two and three words forward is 15.0 percent. These values are greater than the excess branch percentages given in the last section, as they include all branches, not just 8-bit displacement branches. In all cases, these taken branches are required by the architecture and not specified by the program. There are other mechanisms to encode branch displacements. The Motorola M68000 microprocessor uses a special value in a short displacement field to signal that a longer displacement follows. The VAX and PDP-11 already use variable-length instructions and immediate fields. Using the escape mechanism would be a simple change to these architectures.

Optimization significantly reduced the number of executed instructions in the S/370 architecture, but the static size of the programs changed by only 38 percent. Figure 4.6 shows the percentage of taken branches reached by a symmetric displacement. While the S/370 does not use PC-relative branching, this figure calculates the span as if it had half-word (2-byte) offset PC-relative addressing. The Hopt2 and Hopt3 compilers reduce the branch distance by at least a factor of two. Optimizations reduce the static size of often-executed code sequences. For example, the Hopt3 compiler captures 70 percent of the taken branches with a 6-bit displacement. The Fortran G, Hopt1, and Pascal/VS compilers with twice the span (7 bits) are close to and sometimes even well below a 70 percent coverage. The VAX/UNIX and PDP-11 branch coverage would be improved by better optimization. The last chapter showed very similar branch coverages for each architecture when the span and static program size were factored in. Optimization can double the coverage; the magnitude of the improvement often depends on the instruction space savings for short name (ex., registers) vs. long name references.

4.7:   Conclusions

Invariant compiler effects group the language constructs that are not optimized. Control structures exemplify this; the number of conditional control (or branch) points executed by the test work load was within four percent of the CI branch measure. Floating-point operations are also largely invariant with optimization techniques.

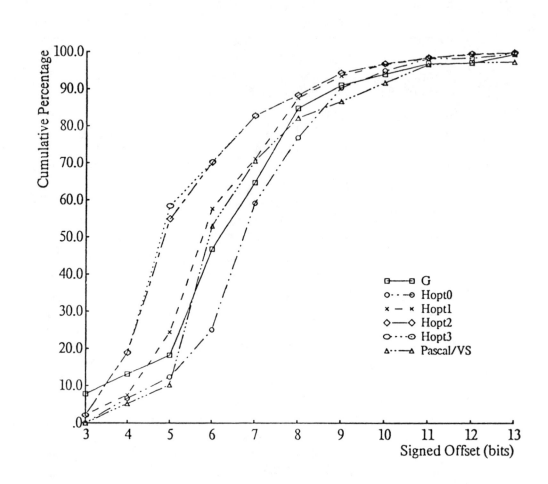

Figure 4.6: S/370 cumulative branch coverage percentage (averages).

Machine-independent effects change the instruction stream and must be carefully considered to ensure fair architectural comparisons. The machine independent effects can totally obscure any true architecture differences. Any efforts to compare architectures must carefully examine the run-time environment and compiler technologies. The next chapter discusses an approach that uses the same run-time environment and compiler for each architecture.

Machine-dependent effects represent true architectural differences. Register allocation by the Fortran Hopt1 compiler reduced the memory requirements to half the initial values.

In a case study of the S/370 compilers, the static program size varied by 38 percent across optimization levels. However, widely different dynamic instruction streams are generated by the six compilers. The dynamic instruction count varies by a factor of 2.8. The instruction stream was broken down to verify invariants and identify the changes. Register allocation is a primary source of change. Further optimizations removed redundant array indexing to reduce the frequency of fixed-point arithmetic calculations. Because the absolute occurrence of invariant instruction classes (branch, floating-point) remained constant, the reduction in total instructions increased the invariants' relative frequency. Branch frequencies increased from 5.3 percent to 15 percent of the instruction stream.

Memory reference behavior also changed because of compiler optimization. The relative importance of array references was increased as the register allocation algorithms assigned simple variables. The frequency of array accesses as indicated by indexed register-to-memory references increased from 14 to 46 percent, while the total number of memory reads and writes decreased by a factor of almost four.

By examining the branch instruction stream, machine independent compiler effects were filtered from the branch data to highlight the excess number of branches by the VAX and PDP-11 architectures. The conditional branch mechanism for these architectures required extra instructions when the branch target exceeded its span. The average branch distance was shown to be halved by compiler optimizations in the S/370 architecture, and thus this could be used to increase the PDP-11 and VAX branch span utilization.

CHAPTER 4. COMPILER EFFECTS

ANALYZING COMPUTER ARCHITECTURES

Chapter 5

Varying Architectures Using a Fixed Compiler Strategy

Chapter 5: Varying Architectures Using a Fixed Compiler Strategy

In the last chapter, we took a single architecture—System 370—and examined its behavior under a variety of different compilation strategies. In this chapter[1] we take a single compiler and, to the extent possible, fix the hardware resources (ALU, cache size, etc.) and examine the effect of purely architectural parameters (formats, register set size, etc.) on overall program behavior.

In the preceding chapters, we studied real machines and actual compilers. This chapter uses an actual compiler to study instruction sets that are purposely normalized—more similar than different. Yet these instruction sets are recognizable relatives—"cousins"—of RISC, S/370, and P-code.

The results in this chapter differ from the earlier chapters in two important ways:

1. They include additional "non-numeric type" benchmarks as well as three of the four scientific benchmarks used in Chapters 3 and 4.

2. They use a recently developed software simulation platform called the *Architect's Workbench*, which is an outgrowth and evolution of the earlier tools developed as part of the Emulation Laboratory [40].

The non-numeric benchmarks are generally more representative of a workstation environment. The size of the program is especially important, as one of the architectural parameters to be studied is the cache size and its performance [13,60].

The purpose of this chapter is to evaluate and compare instruction set designs by using the same compiler strategies and similar implementation constraints.

---

[1]Some of the data (the "non-numeric" benchmarks) in this chapter also appear in a paper by Flynn, Mitchell, and Mulder [23].

5.1:   Modeling Performance in Instruction Set Design

While it is difficult to create a truly fair basis for the comparison of
instruction set designs, our emphasis in this chapter, as in the earlier
chapters, is on performance-oriented considerations. We recognize the
importance of non-performance-oriented considerations, such as functional requirements including compatibility, design time, technology
selection, etc., but these issues are simply beyond the scope of this
book.

5.1.1:   Performance-Oriented Considerations

The CI measures used throughout the earlier chapters are also a basis
for comparison in this chapter. However, the primary objective of this
chapter is to examine architectural parameters, such as the effectiveness
of a certain cache–architecture combination, so that our measurements
are frequently referenced to instruction caches of various sizes or to
register sets of various sizes. In the earlier chapters we could only infer
issues such as cache effectiveness and memory locality from static code
size and required memory bandwidth. Smaller code size is expected
to provide more concise representation and locality in memory. In this
chapter we quantitatively evaluate these issues.

5.1.2:   A Basis for Comparison

We use a single compiler—modifying only the code generation section
to produce different code for the various architectures under consideration and to otherwise normalize processor costs and to examine specific
architectural variations. As has been clear from the preceding chapters, processor–instruction set variations can become lost in the noise
of differences between compilers. This chapter creates a fair-basis comparison for the evaluation of instruction set alternatives by using a
common compile time strategy. Throughout this chapter we assume:

1. Two workloads: the scientific benchmark studied earlier and five
   Pascal benchmarks representative of a non-numeric environment.

2. Relatively simple base instruction sets, including Stack, P-code,
   S/370, and RISC.

3. A fixed implementation technology.

4. A similar level of compiler optimization for all instruction set variations.

5. The same ALU—arithmetic logic unit, data paths, and instruction vocabulary for operations for all instruction set variants (i.e., the same ALU cost).

Instruction count differences arise due only to format, encoding, and register differences.

5.2:   The Benchmarks

Three of the four programs presented in the earlier chapters were run on the Architect's Workbench. The fourth program, Mortran, was omitted due to difficulties in assuring that the I/O would be treated in a way consistent with the results of the Mortran executions in the earlier chapters (this is similar to the VAX/VMS problem cited in Chapter 3). Two of the three programs, FFT and Sort, proved highly susceptible to optimization. The relatively small optimized static sizes of these two programs made it desirable to at least introduce additional benchmark material. Small program sizes can result in exaggerated comparative I-cache performance, as we shall see.

Table 5.1 presents the relevant data for our three scientific benchmarks for a P-code architecture (simple stack architecture) as derived by the AWB compiler with optimization turned off (similar to the "simple compilation" of Chapter 3). The static size for FFT and Sort being on the order of 2kB indicates that even a small I-cache is likely to capture the working sets of these programs and to result in very high hit rates. All data are for the P-code machine with fixed 32-bit instructions. Since the P-code machine is a stack machine, the difference between dynamic size divided by four and instructions is the occurrence of pointers usually associated with procedure calls. The static measure is the program size in bytes as compiled without linkage overhead; it includes only executable code and constants as allowed in the P-code architecture. The percentage of code actually used in the execution of these benchmarks varied from 79 percent to 99 percent.

Table 5.2 compares the number of instructions executed under emulation (Chapter 3) and executed interpretively on the AWB. The AWB U-code compiler was targeted to produce P-code. Both systems used simple or unoptimized, compilers. The percent difference due entirely to the differences in compilers varies from between less than 1 percent up to 9 percent. Larger differences are generally due to the way a particular compiler handles loop constructs [43].

The AWB compiler optimizer can be applied to the P-code machine, resulting in improvements indicated in Table 5.3. The improvements cited represent reductions in size or count. The negative improvement

> **Data Consistency**
> The U-code compiler used by the AWB differs from the compilers used in P-code that produce a P-code object code cited in Chapter 3. These differences are due to the way loops are encoded in a stack machine, and generally range up to 9.1 percent (Table 5.2), with the average somewhat less than 5 percent.

(Norm static size) represents an enlargement of program size. These improvements are not as great as those seen in Chapter 3, because the compiler has been designed to optimize register set type architectures rather than stack architectures. Some of its transformations are simply ineffective in the stack architecture environment.

The non-numeric benchmarks selected for extending this study consist of five Pascal programs originally used by Alpert [4]. They are considerably larger programs in terms of static size, and hence more generally suitable for cache studies.

Some static and dynamic measures for the benchmarks are given in Table 5.4. All data are for a stack machine with fixed 32-bit instructions (P-code). The static measure is the program size in bytes as compiled without linkage overhead; it includes only executable code and constants as allowed in the stack machine architecture [43]. The percentage of code actually used, for the given input files, is between 53 percent and 80 percent.

The CCAL benchmark emulates a desk calculator. It reads a script of calculations from a text file and produces results in another text file. As with the other benchmarks, any input files required are specified as part of the benchmark, thus defining a standard execution. The COMPARE benchmark compares two text files by producing a description of their differences (similar to the UNIX 'diff' command). The PCOMP benchmark compiles a Pascal program by recursive descent and produces P-code output. The PASM benchmark assembles the P-code output from the P-code compiler. The MACRO benchmark is a macro processor for the SCALD computer-aided design system.

The chosen benchmarks are representative Pascal programs of medium size. They represent program generation, file processing and calculation. CCAL also represents an interactive (as opposed to batch) program although it is driven from a script file to keep its execution standard.

Each of these benchmarks was executed once for each target architecture after analysis of its basic blocks; subsequently the address trace of that execution was fed into the cache simulator. The results presented are for the mean of the (equally weighted) benchmarks.

Table 5.1: Scientific benchmarks for stack architecture (P-code) as compiled, unoptimized, by AWB system.

Benchmark	Static Size (Bytes)	% Actually Referenced	Dynamic Size (Bytes)	Instructions (Dynamic)
FFT	2,652	99%	1,875,332	468,112
Sort	1,172	95%	10,155,520	2,538,579
Norm	22,948	79%	15,683,360	3,918,397

Table 5.2: Comparison of dynamic instruction count between emulated P-code (Chapter 3) and interpreted U-code (AWB), unoptimized code.

Benchmark	Emulated P-code*	AWB U-Code	% Difference
FFT	428,949	468,112	9.1%
Sort	2,521,066	2,538,579	0.7%
Norm	3,714,823	3,918,397	5%

* Emulated P-code data from Table 3.14a.

Table 5.3: Instruction size improvement for simple stack (P-code) with compiler optimization (scientific benchmarks).

Improvement:	Static Size	Dynamic Instruction Count
FFT	13%	39%
Sort	3%	3%
Norm	-5%	13%

Table 5.4: Benchmark sizes for a simple stack architecture (P-code).

Benchmark	Static Size (Bytes)	% Actually Referenced	Dynamic Size (Bytes)	Instructions (Dynamic)
CCAL	12,980	63%	4,391,864	1,058,262
COMPARE	8,948	60%	35,113,324	8,538,373
PCOMP	71,276	69%	22,084,724	5,323,939
PASM	15,424	80%	17,814,260	4,352,798
MACRO	73,980	53%	2,538,512	617,765

5.3: The Architectures

In the following analysis, we use four instruction set variants:

1. FIX32; a RISC type architecture. This is a load–store architecture similar to the HP Precision—that is, register file oriented, with FIX32 bit instruction size.

2. OBI360. This instruction set variation is similar to IBM S/370, but excludes the storage to storage instruction format of that instruction set. OBI360 is therefore a RISC strategy, plus: (1) the "RX format" (32 bits), allowing one instruction operand to reside in memory: R1 := R1 op Memory [R2 + offset], and (2) half size (16 bit) register to register instructions: R1 := R1 op R2 (also see note below).

3. A stack machine (P-code) whose instructions have fixed 32-bit size. This is almost identical to our P-code machine.

4. A stack machine (Stack 816) with byte addressability whose instructions with opcode only take one byte, immediate values use 16 bits, and memory reference instructions use 32 bits (four bytes).

5. An implementation of the CI measures called a Direct Correspondence Architecture (DCA). A four-bit prefix is added to each CI instruction to allow 16 formats to realize the CI instruction count.

Table 5.5 summarizes the characteristics of the five test instruction sets. Recall the assumption that all other artifacts remain constant— the base instruction set operational vocabulary, the cycle time, etc. In the next sections we consider the effects of instruction set selection on memory traffic in the presence of various size caches, then we consider the issue of register set size and organization and allocation policy on memory traffic, in the presence of various size caches.

Note: Register set machine operations take two independent source operands (R1 and R2) and place the result in *either* an independent register (R3, the three address convention) *or* one of the source operands (say, R1, the two address convention). Most RISC machines as well as our FIX32 use the former convention, while the IBM System/360 uses the latter. Our code generator was designed to produce three address instructions, but was later modified to produce two address instructions (OBI360). For this code generator and our benchmarks there is little advantage for the independent R3 specification, i.e., the OBI360 data are approximately the same (within 1 percent) for either convention.

Table 5.5: Four instruction sets studied.

Type	Most similar to	Formats	Encoding	Addressability
FIX32	RISC; HP Precision	two basic types: (i) Load R_1, with Mem[addr] or (ii) $R_1 \leftarrow R_2$ op R_3 (all operands in registers)	all instructions occupy 32^b	Word (32^b)
OBI 360	IBM S/370	As with FIX32 plus "RX" type, $R_1 \leftarrow R_1$opMem[Addr]	memory refr instr use 32^b; register refr instr use 16^b and 32^b.	Half word (16^b)
Simple Stack (referred to as P-code)	P-code	Stack formats	All objects occupy 32^b	Word
Stack	typical stack machine	Stack formats	instructions with opcode only 8^b; memory refr instr use 32^b.	Byte
DCA	CI	Direct correspondence with 16 formats; an implementation of a CI architecture.	Bit variable, encoded to CI	Bit

(Also see note on page 156.)

> **The Value of Instruction Code Density**
>
> With the advent of RISC-type architectures, it has become a common belief that simple instruction decoding is a requirement for high performance systems. Those who follow such a dictum pay a significant price for the same performance: twice as much area devoted to instruction cache (and occasionally even more) as an architecture with modest additional attention to code density.
>
> For microprocessors with on-chip cache, it would seem that the best use of area is attention to code density first, and addition of instruction cache area second.

5.4:   The Instruction Stream

Any instruction set is a compromise among competing considerations. A primary tradeoff occurs between instruction complexity and memory traffic. The denser the encoding of an instruction set, the smaller the program representation and the fewer references required to support instruction execution.

For our five instruction sets of interest, we see the effect of encoding on instruction traffic in Figures 5.1–5.5, which show instruction memory traffic relative to OBI360 and Figures 5.6 and 5.7 relative to DCA in the presence of various size instruction caches. The cache size varies from zero bytes (no cache) to an ideal or "infinite" cache. Misses occur in the ideal cache due to the initial loading of the program working set only. The data presented are for a two-way set associative cache with a 16-byte line. Keeping the line size constant normalizes the cost of the instruction cache across all of the four architectures. However, the relatively short line size actually favors the less dense architectures and tends to minimize the differences among the architectures. Naturally the instruction traffic for all of the architectures improves with the addition of a cache, but in analyzing the tradeoff between cache size and instruction set complexity it is important to understand the relative difference among instruction set alternatives; thus, Figures 5.1–5.5 are plotted relative to OBI360 and Figures 5.6 and 5.7 are relative to DCA.

Figure 5.1 shows the performance of an I-cache relative to OBI360 for our RISC, Stack, and P-code machines for the FFT and Sort benchmarks (compiler optimization on). As suspected, the better encoded architecture (OBI360) captures its smaller working set earlier than other architectures and its miss rate goes down relative to these other architectures. This results in relative I-cache performance spikes. The

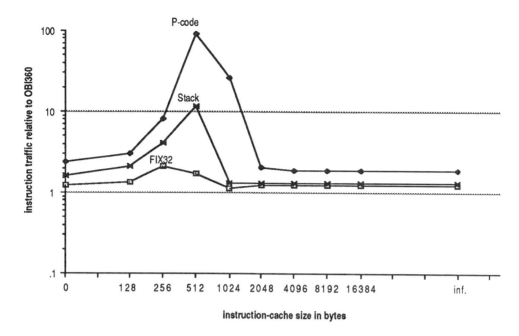

Figure 5.1: Instruction traffic relative to OBI360 for three instruction sets. Benchmarks FFT and Sort, optimization on.

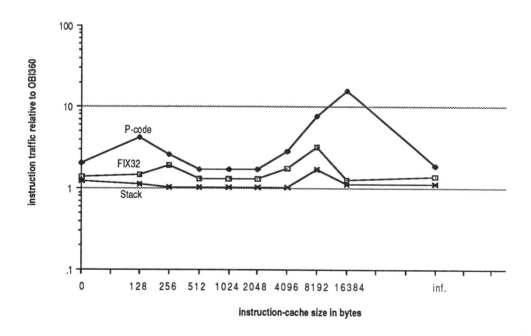

Figure 5.2: Benchmark Norm, optimization on.

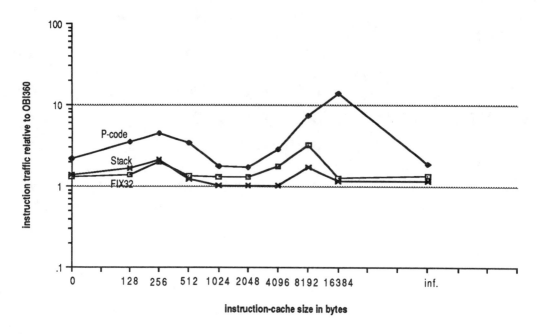

Figure 5.3: Instruction traffic relative to OBI360 for three instruction sets. Three scientific benchmarks, optimization on.

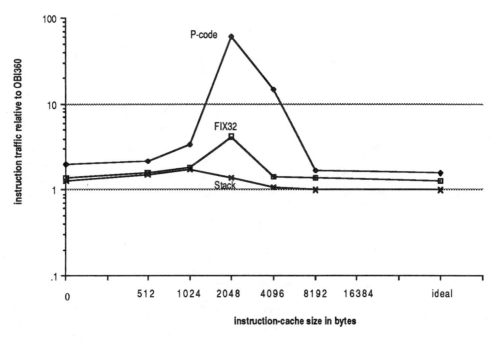

Figure 5.4: Benchmarks FFT and Sort, optimization off.

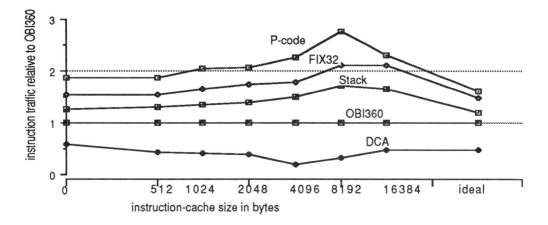

Figure 5.5: Architecture families relative to OBI360 (2-way set associative 16-byte lines). Non-numeric benchmarks, optimization on.

maximum size of the relative spike is interesting and occurs in the region of 256–512 bytes of I-cache:

$$
\begin{array}{lcr}
\text{P-code} & = & 91.7 \\
\text{Stack} & = & 11.5 \\
\text{Fix32} & = & 2.1
\end{array}
$$

Clearly register set machines have an advantage, at least with our compilers, on these benchmarks. Figure 5.2 provides the same information for the larger benchmark Norm (optimization on). Here the maximum spike occurs between 8kB and 16kB:

$$
\begin{array}{lcr}
\text{P-code} & = & 15.9 \\
\text{Stack} & = & 1.7 \\
\text{Fix32} & = & 3.3
\end{array}
$$

Norm is an interesting benchmark, as it exhibits two separate spikes. A smaller spike occurs in the region of 128–256B, which corresponds to the size of one of the more important loops in Norm.

The data from these three benchmarks can be merged as a workload (Figure 5.3); as expected, there are now two pronounced spikes, one corresponding to the loop capture in large benchmarks or program capture for small benchmarks, and the other corresponding to the full working set capture for the larger benchmark. The maximum spike sizes are:

$$
\begin{array}{lcr}
\text{P-code} & = & 13.7 \\
\text{Stack} & = & 2.1 \\
\text{Fix32} & = & 3.2
\end{array}
$$

OBI360

We use our "OBI360" as a better encoding of a RISC machine, since it involves but two coding changes to the RISC-style processor:

1. Addition of the memory-to-register format.

2. The 16-bit register-to-register instruction format.

We use this particular approach to code density simply because it is consistent with the data presented in the earlier chapters, and represents a familiar machine. The case for code density does not begin or end with OBI360. RISC architectures that achieve code density in different ways, e.g., by encoding multiple operations into a single 32-bit instruction, may prove equally effective in achieving a better area tradeoff for microprocessors.

To see the effect of compiler optimization, compare Figure 5.4 with Figure 5.1. Figure 5.4 presents the same relative cache data for the Sort and FFT benchmarks, but with the compiler optimizer turned off. The performance spike now occurs at about 2kB rather that 512B. The optimizer was able to effectively use the register set to reduce the number of instructions (i.e., hold (local) values in registers for use in multiple statements). Stack architectures generally store ("pop") all such results at the end of each statement. Compare the maximum spike sizes for both (relative to OBI360):

	Optimization on:	Optimization off:
P-code	91.7	60.2
Stack	11.5	1.7
Fix32	2.1	4.2

Without optimization, the stack architectures perform relatively better than with optimization. Notable in the above is that without optimization, the simply encoded Fix32 performs poorer than the better encoded Stack. With optimization, the Fix32 significantly outperforms Stack.

Figure 5.5 shows the same data for the five non-numeric benchmarks since these programs are all relatively large (static size) and have approximately the same character. When they are averaged together they should display a single spike relative to OBI360. However, the data represent a convolution of performance measurements for these five programs, and mask the relative spike sizes for the individual programs, which vary from a peak size of 3 to 30:1. Throughout all of these benchmarks, some general conclusions are:

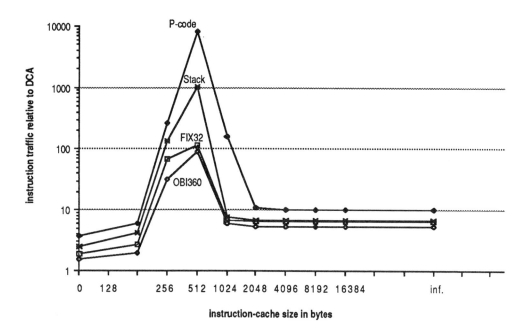

Figure 5.6: Architecture families relative to DCA (approx CI). Benchmarks FFT and Sort, optimization on.

1. Without a cache (i.e., dynamic instruction traffic) the simplest architecture, P-code, requires about twice as much instruction traffic as does the reference, OBI360. Fix32 and Stack require about 1.5 or 50 percent additional instruction traffic over the reference OBI360.

2. For certain intermediate size caches, relative performance is significantly poorer for the least dense architectures. On benchmarks with well defined working sets, relative performance differences of greater than 10:1 are not uncommon.

3. With very large caches, the working set of all architectures is captured and the original relationship is restored since only the initial misses to bring the program into the cache are involved. Even here, the less dense architectures simply require more misses to bring in its program image than a better encoded architecture.

If we used the DCA or the CI approximation as the baseline, the results are further exaggerated, as can be seen in Figure 5.6 for the

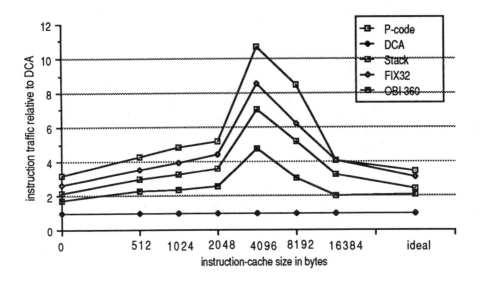

Figure 5.7: Architecture families relative to DCA (approx CI). Non-numeric benchmarks, optimization on.

Table 5.6: I-cache performance of various architectures relative to DCA (realizable CI measures). The first column is relative to the DCA instruction traffic with no cache, non-numeric benchmarks.

DCA	Cache Size	P-Code	Stack	FIX32	OBI360
1.000	0	3.18	2.13	2.61	1.71
.0253	512	4.29	2.94	3.49	2.27
.0152	1^K	4.83	3.22	3.94	2.35
.0087	2^K	5.16	3.58	4.44	2.53
.0026	4^K	10.67	7.05	8.52	4.78
.0013	8^K	8.5	5.19	6.24	3.02
.0007	16^K	4.05	3.21	4.08	2.00
.0004	∞	3.42	2.42	3.08	2.08

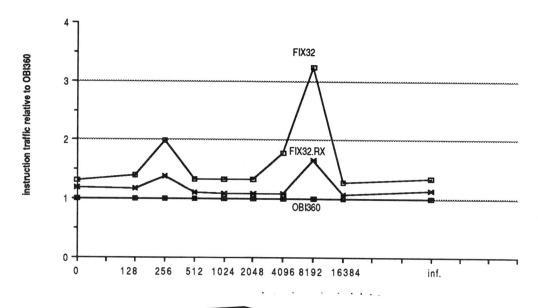

Figure 5.8: Relative instruction traffic for closely related architectures. Three scientific benchmarks, optimization on.

Sort and FFT benchmarks, optimization on. Here the maximum spikes occur between 256 and 512B with relative sizes:

OBI360	=	89.8
Fix32	=	155.1
P-code	=	8,228.7
Stack	=	1,031.1

It is interesting to note that because of the way our compiler generates DCA code for array elements, the data understate the relative differences, especially vis-a-vis register set machines! Similar data are presented in Table 5.6 and Figure 5.7 for the non-numeric benchmarks. Here again, the effect of averaging the five benchmarks broadens the base of the spike and reduces the height.

Since several of our architectures are closely related (OBI360 and Fix32, P-code and Stack) it is interesting to consider these related architectures by themselves. Figure 5.8 (scientific benchmarks—optimization on) and Figure 5.9 (non-numeric benchmarks, optimization on) shows Fix32 relative to OBI360. Recall that OBI360 differs from Fix32 by the addition of

1. Memory to register (the "RX" format in S/360 terms).

2. Half size RR (16-bit) register to register operations.

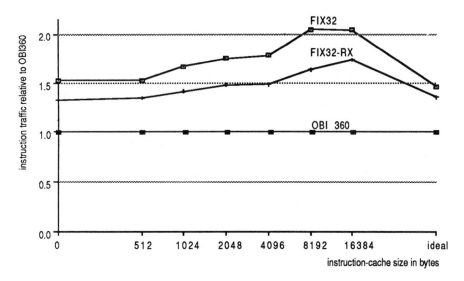

Figure 5.9: Non-numeric benchmarks, optimization on.

With these benchmarks, the addition of the memory to register operation significantly diminishes the size of the spike or the relative cache performance difference between Fix32 and OBI360. The addition of an RX format causes minimal additional decoding complexity. RISC designers have argued against this instruction format on the basis of its disruption of the instruction pipeline. The data here indicate that one could profitably add the RX instruction and *not* disturb the pipeline. That is, to consider the addition of the format simply as an enhancement to the instruction coding density. Of course, if implementation considerations allowed the use of the RX instruction to reduce cycles in program execution, so much the better.

The difference between Fix32 RX and OBI360 then, is the half size register to register instructions. As mentioned in Section 5.3, register set machines take two independent source operands (R1 and R2) and place the result in either an independent register (R3) or one of the source operands (e.g., R1, the three address or two address convention).

For our compiler and benchmarks, the three address convention offered little advantage (compiler optimization on). Thus, the addition of the half size RR instruction depends on two considerations:

1. The limitation on register set size. Given a 16-bit instruction, the half-size RR instruction is limited to 16 or at most 32 registers.

2. Additional hardware expense. The half size RR format requires some additional shifting and multiplexing of data from a 32-bit word to a line 16-bit instructions to enter an instruction decoder.

CHAPTER 5. VARYING ARCHITECTURES

I-Cache Spikes

The relative performance of two architectures with the same size instruction cache may be dramatically different, as evidenced by the spikes in Figures 5.1 through 5.5. All architectures improve with the addition of a cache. Some improve much faster than others—the ones that are better encoded capture their working set first.

I-cache performance, however, is but one of several elements that determine overall processor performance. A large I-cache performance disadvantage certainly will not translate into an overall performance disadvantage of the same size, comparing one architecture to another.

A similar case can be made for Stack relative to a pure 32-bit stack machine as in P-code (see Figures 5.10 and 5.11).

Figures 5.10 and 5.11 show a similar instruction traffic profile for the stack machines. In the Stack architecture the opcodes require only 8 bits and small constants can be contained in 16 bits, otherwise all memory references are, as in the stack machine, 32 bits. Branch targets are byte-aligned.

Tables 5.7 and 5.8 illustrate these differences perhaps even more graphically. To achieve essentially the same miss rate for memory instruction traffic from memory, the more dense architecture (either OBI360 or Stack) requires only half the cache instruction size of the less dense architecture (FIX32 and Stack). Note that with relatively simple hardware additions, the resultant designs for both instruction sets would require significantly smaller caches to realize the same memory traffic.

Table 5.9 compares instruction traffic for our four "cousin" architectures that have been examined in the previous chapters. It includes the CI instruction count for the average programs from Tables 3.14c and d for each of the architectures (excluding Mort). In order to compute the relative instruction bandwidth (in bytes per CI) among the four architectures, we must adjust the CI instruction count by the average instruction size. Both the HP Precision and P-code have fixed instruction size of 32 bits, or 4 bytes. However, System 370 has an average instruction size of 3.35 bytes (simple compile) to 3.54 bytes (optimized compile), from Table 4.19 (without Mort correction). Thus, in order to put it on a comparable basis with the P-code and HP Precision results, the instruction count must be multiplied by the appropriate factor. Notice that the I-bandwidth column is relative instruction traffic in bytes per canonic instruction. For the two compiler strategies, we can now make comparisons and compare these results to those predicted by the Architect's Workbench. The measured relative traffic lies within

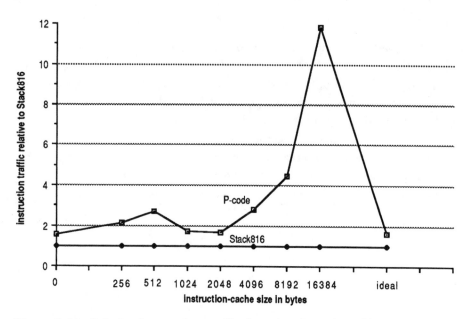

Figure 5.10: Relative instruction traffic for related stack architectures. Three scientific benchmarks, optimization on.

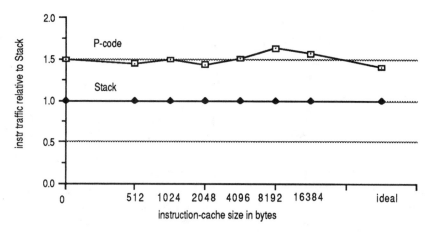

Figure 5.11: Relative instruction traffic for related stack architectures. Non-numeric benchmarks, optimization on.

CHAPTER 5. VARYING ARCHITECTURES

Table 5.7: Relative traffic or miss rates. All traffic is relative to OBI360 without a cache and with 32^b-wide paths to memory.

(a) Scientific benchmarks

For Cache[a] Size:	0	256	512	1^K	4^K	8^K
Fix 32	1.32	.41	.18	.18	.14	.05
Fix 32 RX	1.19	.28	.15	.15	.09	.02
OBI360	1.0	.21	.14	.13	.08	.01

(b) Non-numeric benchmarks

For Cache[a] Size:	0	512	1^K	2^K	4^K
Fix 32	1.52	.44	.30	.19	.11
Fix 32 RX	1.33	.37	.24	.17	.09
OBI360	1.0	.28	.17	.11	.05

[a] Two-way set-associative, 8-byte lines.

Table 5.8: Relative traffic or miss rates. All traffic is relative to Stack (no cache) with 32^b-wide paths to memory.

(a) Scientific benchmarks

For Cache[a] Size:	0	256	512	1^K	4^K	8^K
P-Code	1.56	0.67	0.35	0.17	0.17	.08
Stack	1.0	0.31	0.12	0.10	0.06	.02

(b) Non-numeric benchmarks

For Cache[a] Size:	0	512	1^K	2^K	4^K
P-Code	1.49	0.51	0.35	0.21	0.13
Stack	1.0	0.35	0.23	0.15	0.09

[a] Two-way set-associative, 8-byte lines.

> **Optimization and Stack Machines**
>
> It is interesting to compare Figures 5.1 and 5.4. The better encoded stack machine, Stack, performs better when the compiler optimizer is turned off than Fix32, a RISC machine. Their relative performance is reversed when compiler optimization is turned on. Modern compiler technology effectively uses the register set in the register set architecture by eliminating a large fraction of instructions—load and store type instructions. Compiler technology is less helpful to the stack machine; with only an evaluation stack the Stack machine must use push and pop instructions to move values to and from memory for use from statement to statement.

12 percent of that predicted by the Architect's Workbench. Given the different compilers and simplifications made in the architectural descriptions, this is expected.

5.5:   The Data Stream

Registers serve many functions: They hold temporary values in expression evaluation, they hold variables from statement to statement within a procedure, and they hold constants and pointers. Figure 5.12 illustrates the types of reference to data memory for variable and temporary accesses for Pascal and C programs. In an architecture without registers (such as our stack or P-code machine), 47 percent of the data references would be to temporary storage of intermediate results within expression evaluation. The addition of as few as two or three registers, whether through the top of the stack or use of a register set, basically eliminates these references. Ignoring expression evaluation, the resultant traffic is for extended source variables, variables whose values are carried from statement to statement within a procedure because of their high probability of use. The register allocator is responsible for predicting the optimum assignment of variables to registers. If we define this extended source variable data traffic as unity data traffic, unity data traffic then includes references to variables defined in the source program as well as references to implied data objects, such as compiler-created variables and run-time support.

If we had instruction sets with the same register set size and the same degree of compiler optimization, the resultant traffic would be the same for all instruction sets. Without a data or instruction cache, instruction traffic dominates data traffic but in the presence of even a small instruction cache, data traffic will dominate total traffic (Figures 5.13 and 5.14). In Figure 5.13, both FIX32 and OBI360 instruction

Table 5.9: Instruction traffic for four architectures (three scientific benchmarks).

	Compiler	CI Instr. Count	I-Bytes per CI	OBI360 I-Bw Relative to P-Code	
				Measured	Predicted (AWB)
P-Code	simple	6.02	24.08	1.0	1.0
S/370 (OBI360)	simple	3.39	11.36	0.47	0.53 (12% error)
				FIX32 I-Bw relative to S/360	
				measured	predicted (AWB)
S/370 (OBI360)	optimized	1.76	6.23	1	1
HP Precision (FIX32)	optimized	2.15	8.62	1.38	1.32 (5% error)

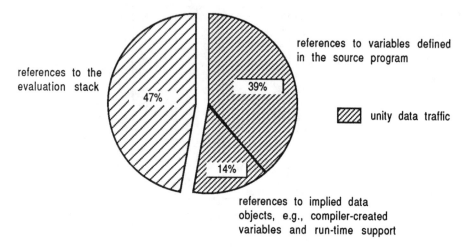

references to variables defined in the source program

references to the evaluation stack

39%

47%

unity data traffic

14%

references to implied data objects, e.g., compiler-created variables and run-time support

Figure 5.12: Distribution of data reference types.

sets have 16 general purpose registers. The addition of an instruction cache reduces the instruction traffic well below the unity data traffic for all architectures, thus there is a need to reexamine the issue of data traffic once a small instruction cache is included in a processor.

5.5.1: Register Sets

Figure 5.15 illustrates the allocation of registers within a typical 16-register set. For unity data traffic, perhaps ten of the registers are used for specified functions and are unavailable to the allocator. Figure 5.16 a presents two allocation strategies. The first is a one–one strategy, where variables are allocated to registers once per procedure (based on predicted usage). The second is a more elaborate many–one strategy that allocates several variables sequentially to the same register within a procedure. This requires the detection of "dead" variables and the reassignment of a register to a new variable. For either type of allocator, making more than eight registers available to this type of allocator has marginal value. The maximum reduction in data traffic is benchmark dependent; between 0.3 and 0.65 of our unity data traffic is achievable with many–one register allocation. To improve data traffic beyond this requires allocation of registers across procedures. This can be done either in software, by interprocedural register allocation, or in hardware, through register windows. Since none of the instruction sets studied or emulated used register windows, this is not further discussed here (but see Mulder [44]).

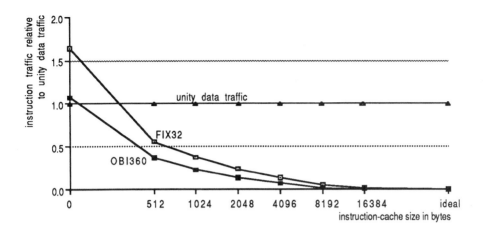

Figure 5.13: Instruction and data traffic as a function of architecture and instruction cache size (non-numeric benchmarks).

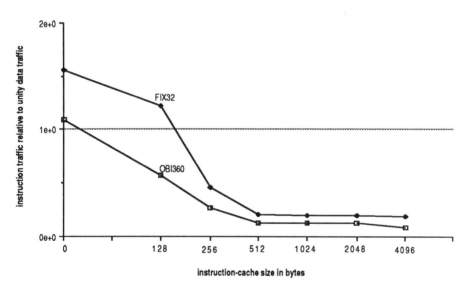

Figure 5.14: Instruction and data traffic as a function of architecture and instruction cache size (three scientific benchmarks).

Table 5.10: Total measured data memory traffic (reads and writes) relative to CI, from Tables 3.25a and b and 3.26a and b.

Architecture	Compiler	Data Memory Traffic Relative to CI	Comments
P-Code	simple	1.11	no reg/only eval.stack
S/370	simple	0.68	16 Reg
S/370	optimized	0.42	16 Reg
HP Precision	optimized	0.37	32 Reg

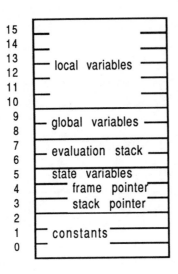

Figure 5.15: A possible register set usage outline.

Table 5.10 presents the data traffic for each of our four architectures relative to CI data traffic. Since the CI data measures include the effect of an evaluation stack, it approximates our unity data traffic. System 370 and the HP Precision have similar data traffic ratios—0.42 references/CI reference and 0.37, respectively. This is what would be expected from Figure 5.16, since the marginal utility of an additional 16 registers is slight. One ought to observe, however, that the variance among the programs is high.

The variation within a single architecture—System 370—caused by compiler strategies is 62 percent (.42/.68). This is generally expected from Figure 5.17, which would predict .38/.70 (many–one/one–one). The large value for P-code is surely a result of the lack of registers to hold local values in the instruction set (i.e., it approximates our unity data traffic).

5.6: Annotated Bibliography

Much of this chapter follows, in outline at least, Flynn *et al.* [23]. That reference also contains the data cited in this chapter for the non-numeric benchmarks. One of the best-known references to cache behavior is Smith [61]. A more complete description of the Architect's Workbench can be found in Mitchell and Flynn [40]. For details on register allocation, the reader is referred to Chaitin [11] and Chow [12].

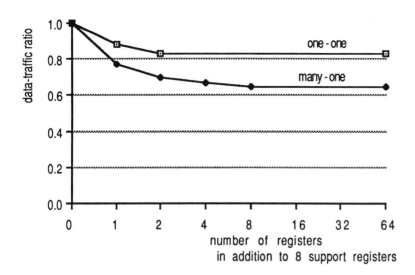

Figure 5.16: Single register set performance relative to unity data traffic (non-numeric benchmarks).

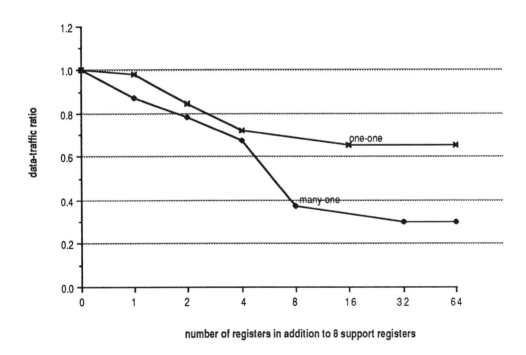

Figure 5.17: Single register set performance relative to unity data traffic (scientific benchmarks).

> **Data Traffic**
>
> Once even a small instruction cache is added to an architecture, the data traffic dominates performance considerations. By the time a processor has 512 bytes or more of instruction cache, it is unlikely that any number of registers or any conventional register allocation scheme will bring the data traffic to a value below that of the instruction traffic; a data cache should be considered at this point.
>
> Data traffic is largely a function of the number of registers available to the processor, and the register allocation scheme used by the compiler, rather than a function of the instruction set architecture itself (except insofar as that instruction set can specify the required number of registers).

5.7: Conclusions

There are many situations where the designer is interested in the analysis of an architectural feature rather than a complete architecture–compiler pair. The effectiveness of a larger register set or larger cache for a particular application is an example. For these situations the intricacies, complexities, and variations among compiler and extraneous instruction set issues tend to mask the essential issues under consideration.

The Architect's Workbench is an efficient software simulator designed to deal with the above situations. The architectures can be normalized to eliminate ALU or data path issues, and a common compiler is used. These synthetic architectures can be made to resemble the basic instruction set of familiar architectures, and generally predict architectural performance to within 10 percent. One can complete the behavioral description of a processor and expect to achieve performance predictions to within 1 percent. However, complete behavioral simulations are time consuming and—more importantly—may not be supported with the software necessary to run large applications. Without this software, evaluations are performed on the basis of small, hand-generated "kernel" programs whose results are controversial, prone to error, and useless for cache or memory evaluation.

The Architect's Workbench approach provides the alternative of easy-to-use approximate architectures evaluated on complete applications for early overall architectural analysis. This contrasts with (and complements) the high-fidelity emulation evaluation discussed in earlier chapters.

ANALYZING COMPUTER ARCHITECTURES

Appendix A

The Sort Program

APPENDIX A. THE SORT PROGRAM

Appendix A: The Sort Program

```
      COMMON N, M, FAIL, X, COUNT, AKEY(100), STACKL(100), STACKR(100)
      INTEGER AKEY, STACKL, STACKR
      INTEGER N, M, FAIL, X, COUNT
      INTEGER I
      N = 100
      M = 12
      COUNT = 0
      FAIL = 0
      X = 0

      DO 10 COUNT=1,100
         CALL SETARR
         CALL SORT
         CALL CHECK
         IF( FAIL .EQ. 1)  WRITE(6,1000)
 1000    FORMAT('SORT FAILED')
 10   CONTINUE
      STOP
      END
CCCCCCCCCCCCCCCCCCCCCCCCCCCCCCCCCCCCCCCCCCCCCCCCCCCCCCCCCC
C
C PROCEDURE SETARR( VAR AKEY: LIST);
C
CCCCCCCCCCCCCCCCCCCCCCCCCCCCCCCCCCCCCCCCCCCCCCCCCCCCCCCCCC
      SUBROUTINE SETARR
      COMMON N, M, FAIL, X, COUNT, AKEY(100), STACKL(100), STACKR(100)
      INTEGER AKEY, STACKL, STACKR
      INTEGER N, M, FAIL, X, COUNT
      DO 10 I = 1, N
         X = MOD( 7855*X + 1731, 8192)
         AKEY(I) = X
 10      CONTINUE
      RETURN
      END
```

```
C
CCCCCCCCCCCCCCCCCCCCCCCCCCCCCCCCCCCCCCCCCCCCCCCCC
C
C PROCEDURE SORT( VAR AKEY: LIST);
C
CCCCCCCCCCCCCCCCCCCCCCCCCCCCCCCCCCCCCCCCCCCCCCCCC
      SUBROUTINE SORT
      COMMON N, M, FAIL, X, COUNT, AKEY(100), STACKL(100), STACKR(100)
      INTEGER AKEY, STACKL, STACKR
      INTEGER N, M, FAIL, X, COUNT
      INTEGER I,J,L,R,XKEY,W,S
      S = 1
      STACKL(1) = 1
      STACKR(1) = 100
30        L = STACKL(S)
          R = STACKR(S)
          S = S - 1
40            I = L
              J = R
              XKEY = AKEY((L + R) / 2)
50            CONTINUE
                  IF (AKEY(I) .GE. XKEY) GOTO 70
60                I = I + 1
                  IF (AKEY(I) .LT. XKEY) GOTO 60
70                CONTINUE
                  IF (XKEY .GE. AKEY(J)) GOTO 90
80                J = J - 1
                  IF (XKEY .LT. AKEY(J)) GOTO 80
90                CONTINUE
                  IF (I .GT. J) GOTO 100
                      W = AKEY(I)
                      AKEY(I) = AKEY(J)
                      AKEY(J) = W
                      I = I + 1
                      J = J - 1
100                   CONTINUE
              IF (I .LE. J) GOTO 50
              IF ((J - L) .GE. (R - I)) GOTO 120
                  IF (I .GE. R) GOTO 110
                      S = S + 1
                      STACKL(S) = I
                      STACKR(S) = R
110                   CONTINUE
                  R = J
                  GOTO 140
120           CONTINUE
                  IF (L .GE. J) GOTO 130
                      S = S + 1
                      STACKL(S) = L
```

APPENDIX A. THE SORT PROGRAM

```
                         STACKR(S) = J
130                  CONTINUE
                 L = I
140                  CONTINUE
          IF (L .LT. R) GOTO 40
       IF (S .NE. 0) GOTO 30
       RETURN
       END
C
CCCCCCCCCCCCCCCCCCCCCCCCCCCCCCCCCCCCCCCCCCCCCCCCCCCC
C
C PROCEDURE CHECK( VAR AKEY: LIST);
C
CCCCCCCCCCCCCCCCCCCCCCCCCCCCCCCCCCCCCCCCCCCCCCCCCCC
       SUBROUTINE CHECK
       COMMON N, M, FAIL, X, COUNT, AKEY(100), STACKL(100), STACKR(100)
       INTEGER AKEY, STACKL, STACKR
       INTEGER N, M, FAIL, X, COUNT
       INTEGER I, NM1
       I = 1
       NM1 = N-1
       DO 10 I=1,NM1
           IF (AKEY(I) .GT. AKEY(I + 1)) FAIL = 1
  10       CONTINUE
       RETURN
       END
```

APPENDIX A. *THE SORT PROGRAM*

Bibliography

[1] *VAX Architecture Reference Manual*. Bedford, MA, 1983. Doc. EK-VAXAR-RM-002.

[2] A. V. Aho and J. D. Ullman. *Principles of Compiler Design*. Addison-Wesley, Reading, MA, 1977.

[3] W. F. Alexander. *How a Programming Language is Used*. Technical Report CSRG-10, University of Toronto, February 1972.

[4] Donald Alpert. *Memory Hierarchies for Directly Executed Language Microprocessors*. PhD thesis, Stanford University, June 1984. CSL-TR-84-260.

[5] Donald Alpert. *A Pascal P-code Interpreter for the Stanford Emmy*. Technical Report CSL-TR-79-164, Computer Systems Laboratory, Stanford University, September 1979.

[6] G. M. Amdahl, G. A. Blaauw, and F. P. Brooks, Jr. Architecture of the IBM System/360. *IBM Journal of Research and Development*, 8(2):87–101, April 1964.

[7] M. Auslander and M. Hopkins. An overview of the PL.8 compiler. In *SIGPLAN Symposium on Compiler Construction*, pages 22–31, June 1982.

[8] Mario R. Barbacci. Instruction set processor specifications (ISPS): the notation and its applications. *IEEE Transactions on Computers*, C-30(1):24–40, January 1981.

[9] Joel S. Birnbaum and William S. Worley, Jr. Beyond RISC: high-precision architecture. *Hewlett-Packard Journal*, 36, August 1985.

[10] W. C. Brantley and J. Weiss. A Fortran optimized machine—a high performance, high level language machine. In *Proceedings, International Workshop on High-Level Language Computer Architecture*, University of Maryland, Colleger Park, MD, November 1982.

[11] G. J. Chaitin, M. A. Auslander, A. K. Chandra, J. Cocke, M. E. Hopkins, and P. W. Markstein. Register allocation via coloring. *Computer Languages*, 6:47–57, 1981.

[12] F. Chow and J. Hennessy. Register allocation by priority-based coloring. In *Proceedings of the SIGPLAN'86 Symposium on Compiler Construction*, pages 222–232, ACM, June 1984. Montreal, Canada.

[13] D. W. Clark. Cache performance in the VAX-11/780. *ACM Transactions on Computing Systems*, 1(1):24–37, Feb 1983.

[14] D. W. Clark. Measurement and analysis of instruction use in the VAX 11/780. In *Proceedings of the 9th Annual Symposium on Computer Architecture*, pages 9–17, IEEE Computer Society Press, Washington, DC, April 1982.

[15] D. W. Clark, P. J. Bannon, and J. B. Keller. Measuring VAX 8800 performance with a histogram hardware monitor. In *15th Annual International Symposium on Computer Architecture*, pages 176–185, June 1988.

[16] D. W. Clark and J. S. Emer. Performance of the VAX-11/780 translation buffer: simulation and measurement. *ACM Transactions on Computing Systems*, 3(1):31–62, February 1985.

[17] W. Connors, V. Mercer, and T. Sorlini. *S/360 Instruction Usage Distribution*. Technical Report TR 00.2025, IBM, May 1970.

[18] W. B. Dietz and L. Szewerenko. Architectural efficiency measures: an overview of three studies. *Computer*, 12(4):26–33, April 1979.

[19] D. Ditzel and R. McLellan. Register allocation for free: the C machine stack cache. In *Proceedings of the Symposium on Architectural Support for Programming Languages and Operating Systems*, pages 48–56, ACM, Inc., New York, March 1982.

[20] J. L. Elshoff. An analysis of some commercial PL/I programs. *IEEE Transactions on Software Engineering*, SE-2(2):113–120, June 1976.

[21] M. J. Flynn and L. W. Hoevel. *A Theory of Interpretive Architectures: Ideal Language Machines*. Technical Report 170, Computer Systems Laboratory, Stanford University, February 1979.

[22] Michael J. Flynn. Directions and issues in architecture and language. *Computer*, 13(10):5–22, October 1980.

[23] Michael J. Flynn, Chad L. Mitchell, and Johannes M. Mulder. And now a case for more complex instruction sets. *Computer*, 20(9):71–83, September 1987.

[24] C. Foster and R. Gonter. Conditional interpretation of opcodes. *IEEE Transactions on Computers*, C-20(1):108–111, January 1971.

[25] S. Fuller and W. Burr. Measurement and evaluation of alternative computer architectures. *Computer*, 10(10):24–35, October 1977.

[26] J. C. Gibson. *The Gibson Mix*. Technical Report TR 00.2043, IBM Systems Development Division, Poughkeepsie, N.Y., 1970.

[27] R. H. Gonter. *Comparison of the Gibson mix with the UMASS mix*. Technical Report TN/RCC/004, University of Massachusetts, Amherst, MA, November 1969.

[28] R. D. Grappel and J. E. Hemenway. A tale of four μPs: benchmarks quantify performance. *EDN*, 26(7):179–265, April 1 1981.

[29] D. Hammerstrom. *Analysis of Memory Addressing Architecture*. PhD thesis, University of Illinois, Urbana, IL, July 1977.

[30] J. L. Hennessy, N. Jouppi, F. Baskett, and J. Gill. MIPS: a VLSI processor architecture. In *Proceedings, CMU Conference on VLSI Systems and Computations*, pages 337–346, October 1981.

[31] *Precision Architectures manual*. Hewlett-Packard, preliminary edition, 1987.

[32] L. W. Hoevel and M. J. Flynn. *A Theory of Interpretive Architectures: Some notes on DEL design and a FORTRAN Case Study*. Technical Report 170, Computer Systems Laboratory, Stanford University, Stanford, CA, February 1979.

[33] Lee W. Hoevel. *DELtran Principles of Operation: A Directly Executed Language for FORTRAN-II*. Technical Note CSL-TN-77-108, Computer Systems Laboratory, Stanford University, March 1977.

[34] J. C. Huck. *A Virtual Input/Output System for the Stanford Emmy: V-access*. Technical Note 144, Computer Systems Laboratory, Stanford University, Stanford, CA, May 1979.

[35] J. C. Huck and C. J. Neuhauser. I/O device emulation in the Stanford Emulation laboratory. In *Proceedings of Micro 12*, pages 101–108, IEEE Computer Society Press, Washington, D.C., November 1979.

[36] Jerome C. Huck and Michael J. Flynn. Comparative analysis of computer architectures. In *IFIP Congress Proceedings*, Paris, September 1983.

[37] R. K. Johnsson and J. D. Wick. An overview of the Mesa processor architecture. In *Proceedings, Symposium on Architectural Support for Programming Languages and Operating Systems*, pages 20–29, ACM, Inc., New York, March 1982.

[38] B. W. Kernighan and D. M. Ritchie. *The C Programming Language.* Prentice-Hall, 1978.

[39] D. Knuth. *An Empirical Study of Fortran Programs.* Technical Report STAN-CS-70-186, Computer Science Department, Stanford University, Stanford, CA, 1970.

[40] Chad L. Mitchell and Michael J. Flynn. A workbench for computer architects. *IEEE Design & Test*, 5(1):19–29, February 1988.

[41] A. Lunde. *Evaluation of Instruction Set Processor Architectures by Program Tracing.* PhD thesis, Carnegie-Mellon University, June 1974.

[42] M. J. Mahon, *et al.* Hewlett-Packard Precision Architecture: the processor. *Hewlett-Packard Journal*, 37(8):4–21, August 1986.

[43] Chad L. Mitchell. *Processor Architecture and Cache Performance.* PhD thesis, Stanford University, June 1986. CSL-TR-86-296.

[44] Johannes M. Mulder. *Tradeoffs in Data-Buffer and Processor-Architecture Design.* PhD thesis, Stanford University, December 1987.

[45] C. J. Neuhauser. *An Emmy Based PDP-11/20 Emulation.* Technical Report 110, Computer Systems Laboratory, Stanford University, Stanford, CA, March 1977.

[46] C. J. Neuhauser. *Emmy System Peripherals—Principles of Operation.* Technical Note 77, Computer Systems Laboratory, Stanford University, Stanford, CA, December 1975.

[47] C. J. Neuhauser. *Emmy System Processor—Principles of Operation.* Technical Note 114, Computer Systems Laboratory, Stanford University, Stanford, CA, May 1977.

[48] C. J. Neuhauser. *An Emulation Based Analysis of Computer Architecture.* PhD thesis, Johns Hopkins University, Baltimore, MD, 1980.

[49] Peter Nye. *U-Code An Intermediate Language for Pascal* and Fortran*. S-1 Document SAIL-8, Stanford University, May 1982.

[50] D. A. Patterson and C. H. Sequin. A VLSI RISC. *Computer*, 15(9):8–21, September 1982.

[51] M. L. De Prycker. On the development of a measurement system for high level language program statistics. *IEEE Transactions on Computers*, C-31(9):883–891, September 1982.

[52] G. Radin. The 801 minicomputer. In *Proceedings, Symposium on Architectural Support for Programming Languages and Operating Systems*, pages 39–77, ACM, Inc., New York, March 1982.

[53] B. Randell and L. J. Russell. Algol 60 implementation. In *APIC Studies in Data Processing*, Academic Press, Orlando, FL, 1964.

[54] E. L. Robertson. Code generation and storage allocation for machines with span-dependent instructions. *ACM Transactions on Programming Languages and Systems*, 1(1):71–83, July 1979.

[55] S. K. Robinson and I. S. Torsun. An empirical analysis of Fortran programs. *The Computer Journal*, 19(1):56–62, February 1976.

[56] G. Rossmann and B. Rau. System 360 program statistics, internal report. January 1974.

[57] R. G. Scarborough and H. G. Kolsky. Improved optimization of Fortran object programs. *IBM Journal of Research and Development*, 24(6):660–676, November 1980.

[58] M. Shih. *Emmy/Unibus Interface Design Specification*. Technical Note 109, Computer Systems Laboratory, Stanford University, Stanford, CA, January 1977.

[59] L. J. Shustek. *Analysis and Performance of Computer Instruction Sets*. PhD thesis, Stanford University, Stanford, CA, May 1978.

[60] Alan J. Smith. Cache evaluation and the impact of workload choice. In *Proceedings of the 12th International Symposium on Computer Architecture*, pages 64–73, June 1985.

[61] Alan Jay Smith. Cache memories. *Computing Surveys*, 14(3):473–530, September 1982.

[62] H. S. Stone and M. Sutherland. *Interim Final Report: Studies in microprocessors: Results of Statistical Analysis*. Technical Report, University of Massachusetts, Amherst, MA, January 1981.

[63] R. E. Sweet. *Empirical Estimates of Program Entropy.* PhD thesis, Stanford University, Stanford, CA, December 1976.

[64] R. E. Sweet. Static analysis of the Mesa instruction set. In *Proceedings, Symposium on Architectural Support for Programming Languages and Operating Systems,* pages 158–166, ACM, Inc., New York, March 1982.

[65] T. Szymanski. Assembling code for span dependent instructions. *Communications of the ACM,* 21(4):300–308, April 1978.

[66] A. S. Tanenbaum. Implications of structured programming for machine architecture. *Communications of the ACM,* 21(3):237–246, March 1978.

[67] Scott Wakefield. *Studies in Execution Architectures.* PhD thesis, Stanford University, January 1983. CSL-TR-83-237.

[68] Scott Wakefield. *Studies in Execution Architectures.* Technical Report CSL-83-237, Computer Systems Laboratory, Stanford University, January 1983.

[69] W. Wallach. *EMMY/360 Functional Characteristics.* Technical Report 114, Computer Systems Laboratory, Stanford University, Stanford, CA, June 1976.

[70] B. A. Wichmann. *Algol 60 Compilation and Assessment.* Academic Press, Orlando, FL, 1973.

[71] B. A. Wichmann. *Some Statistics from ALGOL Programs.* Technical Report Report CCU11, National Physical Laboratory, England, 1970.

[72] C. Wiecek. A case study of VAX-11 instruction set usage for compiler execution. In *Proceedings, Symposium on Architectural Support for Programming Languages and Operating Systems,* pages 177–184, ACM, Inc., New York, March 1982.

[73] R. Winder. A data base for computer performance evaluation. *Computer,* 6(3):25–29, March 1973.

[74] D. B. Wortman. *A Study of Language Directed Computer Design.* PhD thesis, Stanford University, Stanford, CA, December 1972.

IEEE Computer Society Press

Publications Activities Board

Vice President: Duncan Lawrie, University of Illinois
James Aylor, University of Virginia
P. Bruce Berra, Syracuse University
Jon T. Butler, US Naval Postgraduate School
Tom Cain, University of Pittsburgh
Michael Evangelist, MCC
Eugene Falken, IEEE Computer Society Press
Lansing Hatfield, Lawrence Livermore National Laboratory
Ronald G. Hoelzeman, University of Pittsburgh
Ez Nahouraii, IBM
Guylaine Pollock, Sandia National Laboratories
Charles B. Silio, University of Maryland
Ronald D. Williams, University of Virginia

Editor-in-Chief: Ez Nahouraii, IBM
Editors: Jon T. Butler, US Naval Postgraduate School
Garry R. Kampen, Seattle University
Krishna Kavi, University of Texas, Arlington
Augustin K. Lai, IBM/ROLM Systems
Arnold C. Meltzer, George Washington University
Frederick R. Petry, Tulane University
Charles Richter, MCC
Sol Shatz, The University of Illinois, Chicago
Kit Tham, Mentor Graphics Corporation
Rao Vemuri, University of California, Davis

T. Michael Elliott, Executive Director
Eugene Falken, Publisher
Margaret J. Brown, Managing Editor
(Tutorials and Monographs)
Denise Felix, Production Coordinator (Reprint Collections)
Janet Harward, Promotions Production Manager

Submission of proposals: For guidelines on preparing CS Press Books, write Editor-in-Chief, IEEE Computer Society, 1730 Massachusetts Avenue, N.W., Washington, DC 20036-1903 (telephone 202-371-1012).

Offices of the IEEE Computer Society

Headquarters Office
1730 Massachusetts Avenue, N.W.
Washington, DC 20036-1903
Phone: (202)371-1012
Telex: 7108250437 IEEE COMPSO

Publications Office
10662 Los Vaqueros Circle
Los Alamitos, CA 90720
Membership and General Information: (714)821-8380
Publications Orders: (800)272-6657

European Office
13, Avenue de l'Aquilon
B-1200 Brussels, Belgium
Phone: 32 (2) 770-21-96 Telex: 25387 AWALB

Asian Office
Ooshima Building
2-19-1 Minami-Aoyama, Minato-ku
Tokyo 107, Japan

IEEE Computer Society Press Publications

Monographs: A monograph is a collection of original material assembled as a coherent package. It is typically a treatise on a small area of learning and may include the collection of knowledge gathered over the lifetime of the authors.

Tutorials: A tutorial is a collection of original materials prepared by the editors and reprints of the best articles published in a subject area. They must contain at least five percent original materials (15 to 20 percent original materials is recommended).

Reprint Books: A reprint book is a collection of reprints that are divided into sections with a preface, table of contents, and section introductions that discuss the reprints and why they were selected. It contains less than five percent original material.

Technology Series: The technology series is a collection of anthologies of reprints each with a narrow focus of a subset on a particular discipline.

Purpose
The IEEE Computer Society advances the theory and practice of computer science and engineering, promotes the exchange of technical information among 97,000 members worldwide, and provides a wide range of services to members and nonmembers.

Membership
Members receive the acclaimed monthly magazine *Computer*, discounts, and opportunities to serve (all activities are led by volunteer members). Membership is open to all IEEE members, affiliate society members, and others seriously interested in the computer field.

Publications and Activities
Computer. An authoritative, easy-to-read magazine containing tutorial and in-depth articles on topics across the computer field, plus news, conferences, calendar, interviews, and new products.
Periodicals. The society publishes six magazines and four research transactions. Refer to membership application or request information as noted above.
Conference Proceedings, Tutorial Texts, Standards Documents. The Computer Society Press publishes more than 100 titles every year.
Standards Working Groups. Over 100 of these groups produce IEEE standards used throughout the industrial world.
Technical Committees. Over 30 TCs publish newsletters, provide interaction with peers in specialty areas, and directly influence standards, conferences, and education.
Conferences/Education. The society holds about 100 conferences each year and sponsors many educational activities, including computing science accreditation.
Chapters. Regular and student chapters worldwide provide the opportunity to interact with colleagues, hear technical experts, and serve the local professional community.

Ombudsman
Members experiencing problems — magazine delivery, membership status, or unresolved complaints — may write to the ombudsman at the Publications Office.

Other IEEE Computer Society Press Texts

Monographs

Integrating Design and Test: Using CAE Tools for ATE Programming:
Written by K.P. Parker
(ISBN 0-8186-8788-6 (case)); 160 pages

JSP and JSD: The Jackson Approach to Software Development (Second Edition)
Written by J.R. Cameron
(ISBN 0-8186-8858-0 (case)); 560 pages

National Computer Policies
Written by Ben G. Matley and Thomas A. McDannold
(ISBN 0-8186-8784-3 (case)); 192 pages

Physical Level Interfaces and Protocols
Written by Uyless Black
(ISBN 0-8186-8824-6 (case)); 240 pages

Protecting Your Proprietary Rights in the Computer and High Technology Industries
Written by Tobey B. Marzouk, Esq.
(ISBN 0-8186-8754-1 (case)); 224 pages

Tutorials

Ada Programming Language
Edited by S.H. Saib and R.E. Fritz
(ISBN 0-8186-0456-5); 548 pages

Advanced Computer Architecture
Edited by D.P. Agrawal
(ISBN 0-8186-0667-3); 400 pages

Advanced Microprocessors and High-Level Language Computer Architectures
Edited by V. Milutinovic
(ISBN 0-8186-0623-1); 608 pages

Communication and Networking Protocols
Edited by S.S. Lam
(ISBN 0-8186-0582-0); 500 pages

Computer Architecture
Edited by D.D. Gajski, V.M. Milutinovic, H.J. Siegel, and B.P. Furht
(ISBN 0-8186-0704-1); 602 pages

Computer Communications: Architectures, Protocols and Standards (Second Edition)
Edited by William Stallings
(ISBN 0-8186-0790-4); 448 pages

Computer Grahics (2nd Edition)
Edited by J.C. Beatty and K.S. Booth
(ISBN 0-8186-0425-5); 576 pages

Computer Graphics Hardware: Image Generation and Display
Edited by H.K. Reghbati and A.Y.C. Lee
(ISBN 0-8186-0753-X); 384 pages

Computer Grahics: Image Synthesis
Edited by Kenneth Joy, Max Nelson, Charles Grant, and Lansing Hatfield
(ISBN 0-8186-8854-8 (case)); 384 pages

Computer and Network Security
Edited by M.D. Abrams and H.J. Podell
(ISBN 0-8186-0756-4); 448 pages

Computer Networks (4th Edition)
Edited by M.D. Abrams and I.W. Cotton
(ISBN 0-8186-0568-5); 512 pages

Computer Text Recognition and Error Correction
Edited by S.N. Srihari
(ISBN 0-8186-0579-0); 364 pages

Computers for Artificial Intelligence Applications
Edited by B. Wah and G.-J. Li
(ISBN 0-8186-0706-8); 656 pages

Database Management
Edited by J.A. Larson
(ISBN 0-8186-0714-9); 448 pages

Digital Image Processing and Analysis: Volume 1: Digital Image Processing
Edited by R. Chellappa and A.A. Sawchuk
(ISBN 0-8186-0665-7); 736 pages

Digital Image Processing and Analysis: Volume 2: Digital Image Analysis
Edited by R. Chellappa and A.A. Sawchuk
(ISBN 0-8186-0666-5); 670 pages

Digital Private Branch Exchanges (PBXs)
Edited by E.R. Coover
(ISBN 0-8186-0829-3); 400 pages

Distributed Control (2nd Edition)
Edited by R.E. Larson, P.L. McEntire, and J.G. O'Reilly
(ISBN 0-8186-0451-4); 382 pages

Distributed Database Management
Edited by J.A. Larson and S. Rahimi
(ISBN 0-8186-0575-8); 580 pages

Distributed-Software Engineering
Edited by S.M. Shatz and J.-P. Wang
(ISBN 0-8186-8856-4 (case)); 304 pages

DSP-Based Testing of Analog and Mixed-Signal Circuits
Edited by M. Mahoney
(ISBN 0-8186-0785-8); 272 pages

End User Facilities in the 1980's
Edited by J.A. Larson
(ISBN 0-8186-0449-2); 526 pages

Fault-Tolerant Computing
Edited by V.P. Nelson and B.D. Carroll
(ISBN 0-8186-0677-0 (paper) 0-8186-8667-4 (case)); 432 pages

Gallium Arsenide Computer Design
Edited by V.M. Milutinovic and D.A. Fura
(ISBN 0-8184-0795-5); 368 pages

Human Factors in Software Development (Second Edition)
Edited by B. Curtis
(ISBN 0-8186-0577-4); 736 pages

Integrated Services Digital Networks (ISDN) (Second Edition)
Edited by W. Stallings
(ISBN 0-8186-0823-4); 404 pages

For Further Information:

IEEE Computer Society, 10662 Los Vaqueros Circle, Los Alamitos, CA 90720

IEEE Computer Society, 13, Avenue de l'Aquilon, 2, B-1200 Brussels, BELGIUM

IEEE Computer Society, Ooshima Building, 2-19-1 Minami-Aoyama, Minato-ku, Tokyo 107, JAPAN